The Colonial Silversmith

The research for this book was partially supported
by a grant from the American Philosophical Society

The Colonial Silversmith

His Techniques & His Products

Henry J. Kauffman

Professor, Industrial Arts Education
Millersville State College
Millersville, Pa.

Drawings by
Dorothy Briggs
Staff Artist
Smithsonian Institution
Washington, D.C.

Galahad Books
New York

Design by Harold Leach

Library of Congress Catalog Card Number: 73-90836
ISBN 0-88365-136-X

Printed in the United States of America

Acknowledgments

Writing this part of the book is doubtless the most pleasant part of such a survey. Pleasant, not only because it is evidence that long hours of research and writing have been completed, but also because it gives the author an opportunity to thank the various people and organizations for their help in assembling the contents of the book.

Work that has been done over a long period of time does not permit the author to keep a perfect record of all who have made numerous contributions. I do want to especially thank Samuel Kirk & Son, Inc., Colonial Williamsburg, and The Henry Francis du Pont Winterthur Museum for the invaluable suggestions they have given the author and for making their facilities for research available to him. In addition, the following people have rendered unstinting help on many occasions: Mrs. Louise Belden, Miss Helen Belknap, Howard T. Brenner, Alfred Clegg, Paul Day, Philip Hammerslough, Frank Horton, Charles Hummel, Joe Kindig, Jr., Ian Quimby, Kenneth Roberts, and John Rouse.

Finally, I would like to emphasize that the unique contents of the book are the attractive drawings made by Dorothy Briggs. Her knowledge of technical drafting, her aesthetic sensitivity, and her tireless patience in dealing with the minutia of the drawings, are fully appreciated by the author.

The inevitable errors in a survey of this type are the responsibility of the author who will be grateful for corrections and constructive criticisms.

Contents

The Colonial Silversmith

William Plumsted is Dr
mo 14
21 to a pepper Caster wt 5:8 fash:ⁿ   1: 0 —

Recᵈ of Francis Richardson 46:4 of
Silver to be made into Buckels —

William Logan is Dr —
23 to a pr of Garter Buckels w 12:21   0 - 10 - 6

Recᵈ of Samuel Shoe Maker 9:9 of
Silver to be made into a pr of Casters

Recᵈ of Ozwel Peal 20:9 of
Silver to Be made into a Tankard
& 16:1:12 of Do to be made into a Poringer

Ozwel Peal is Dr to a Gold Stay
hook w 4:21 — — — — — —   0: 19 - 6

Jeremiah Warder is Dr
th
25 to 6 Spoons w 11:3:16 — —   5: 18 - 6

Anthony Duche is Dr
to 4 Silver Spoons w 7:6 at 9/0 —   3: 5 - 8
to makeing the above Spoons   0 - 12 —

Rebecca Coleman is Dr to two
st
31 Poringers — w 12:14:12   for: 1 - 4 —

Ozwel Peal is Dr
31 to two Poringers w 15:6:12   fashion 1: 4

Introduction

Every book has its *raison d'être*, in some cases evident and easily recognized, in others subtle and difficult to discern. One author wishes to bring a new discovery into sharper focus, another to preserve knowledge of the past which will probably be important to posterity.

The purpose of the present volume is to record and thereby to preserve information about the tools, materials, techniques, and products of the silver trade in America in the eighteenth century. During that period, goods were made almost entirely by hand methods, although the lathe was probably present in the shops of a few silversmiths. *The Colonial Silversmith* is an account of the production of useful objects from silver.

In the past, research has followed traditional patterns, emphasizing historic style, regional differences, and the names and genealogy of craftsmen, and owners, but making only limited comment regarding such matters as materials, tools, and techniques. As a result, most experts know that John Coney was one of the first important silversmiths working in America, but their knowledge of the metallurgy of silver is very meager. Unfortunately, there has been not only a dearth of knowledge about such matters, but even misinformation.

Today, of course, new importance is being attached to metals and their fabrication. The tremendous utilization of metals in contemporary life has increased people's interest, which, in turn, has aroused curiosity about the metal technology of the past. Scholars, researchers, and antiquarians now are beginning to realize that a knowledge of materials and modes of manufacture can aid in determining when, where, how, and why an object was made; this insight can also help them to integrate the relation-

Page from a day book (1744-1748) of Joseph Richardson of Philadelphia. Some entries document the fact that patrons provided the silver to be wrought into specific objects for them. *Courtesy Historical Society of Pennsylvania.*

ships of such data with other facets of life in the past. In addition, the possession of this heretofore obscure information will assist many craftsmen in creating objects of metal by hand methods, and in experiencing the satisfaction which comes from producing an object personally—an experience all too rare in the mid-twentieth century.

The perceptive reader of this book will doubtless make comparisons between the old methods and contemporary ones, a practice that could

Entries in the day book of Joseph Richardson, Jr., of Philadelphia in 1797 indicate that he was in the wholesale business by today's standards. Apparently it was very fashionable to have eagles engraved on arm bands at that time. *Courtesy Historical Society of Pennsylvania.*

𝕯𝖎𝖊𝖉,

In this borough, on Friday evening, the 29th ult after an illness of two days, in the 47th year of his age, Mr. PETER GETZ, the original improver of the new printing-press, constructed with rollers in lieu of a screw.

He was famous for his ingenuity.

arouse in the injudicious a feeling of contempt for old methods which were followed longer in America than in Europe because the so-called "scientific era" was slow in coming here. While Savery, Newcomen, and Watt could give their full time to battling the technological problems of the steam engine, Americans were busy fighting Indians, building relatively primitive shelters, and wresting the fare for their tables from a rich but elusive store on land and sea. In addition, our craftsmen were restricted by the system of English mercantilism, which discouraged the manufacturing of badly needed objects of metal.

Nevertheless, it must be realized that however unfavorable conditions were here for manufacturing ("making by hand"), many craftsmen were busy at their benches throughout the eighteenth century. Their newspaper advertisements attest to the fact that a competitive economy was slowly arising and producing such outstanding results that even experts often have difficulty in determining whether certain objects were made here or in Europe. However, although a distinctive style slowly emerged in the eighteenth century, the problem of identification was compounded by the fact that metals, regardless of where they were mined and refined, rarely have unique or distinctive characteristics.

Whatever may be the state of the reading public's knowledge of such historical matters, its information about metallurgy and technology is perhaps scantier. It may be assumed, however, that most readers know that, although the properties of various metals frequently differ, they often have certain common properties. For example, most metals are heavy and hard, some are inert, others deteriorate rapidly, and still others can be combined to form "alloys."

To be Sold, by Public Vendue,

On Wednesday, the 8th August next,

AT the late residence of Peter Getz, deceased, in South Queen-street, the following articles, viz : —

A COMPLETE

TURNER'S LATH,

with all the necessary apparatus, in the best of order ; a *smith's vice,* nearly new ; files of every description, with a variety of other articles, superfluous to mention in an advertisement.

The sale will commence at 10 o'clock in the forenoon. Attendance will be given by

CHARLES REISINGER, *Adm'r.*

July 23, 1810.   10–2oq.

Notice of the Public Vendue of a complete turner's lathe in the *Lancaster Journal,* July 23, 1810. Getz was a very versatile craftsman and used the lathe for his work in silver as well as the many other pursuits he followed.

The alloys were created to obtain qualities not found in a single element. Thus, pure silver is relatively soft and has few commercial uses, but when a small percentage of copper is added a reasonably tough and useful alloy is created.

In many ways man has adapted and formed metals for his use and welfare. He has learned that metals can be softened into liquid by heating, a quality called "fusibility." Man has further discovered that, when hot metals are cooled, they can be solidified in the shape he chooses, a process known as casting.

Another of man's discoveries is that metals can be changed into various shapes by hammering (extended in length or width and proportionally reduced in thickness) when they are either hot or cold. This quality is called "malleability." Since silver is quite malleable, most objects of this metal are products of the hammer.

Man has also bent or drawn metals into desired shapes when hot or cold. This quality is called "ductility." Metals with a high degree of ductility can be drawn into thin wires, gold being the highest and silver second in this property.

In addition to these methods of altering the shape of a single piece of metal, pieces can be joined together in many ways with or without the application of heat. Two pieces of iron, heated to a "pasty" condition, can be welded together with a hammer without the use of a flux (cleaning agent) or solder. This procedure was used extensively by colonial craftsmen and is known as "welding."

Objects consisting of more than one part were frequently joined by solder, which has a lower melting point than that of the metals to be joined. Thus, by applying heat with a soldering iron or a forge fire, the various parts of an assemblage could be more or less permanently joined. All soldering operations require a flux to keep the metal clean and to allow the solder to flow throughout the joint.

Another device, the rivet, was often used to join parts made of copper, brass, tin, and iron, but rarely employed on objects of silver. Handles of wood were attached to objects of metal by inserting a tennon into a ferrule and securing the two parts by inserting a pin.

A brief summation of data such as this, of course, makes no pretense of being complete, but it can supply the reader with an insight into some of the mysteries of the world of metals. Additional data will be supplied as the need appears throughout the book.

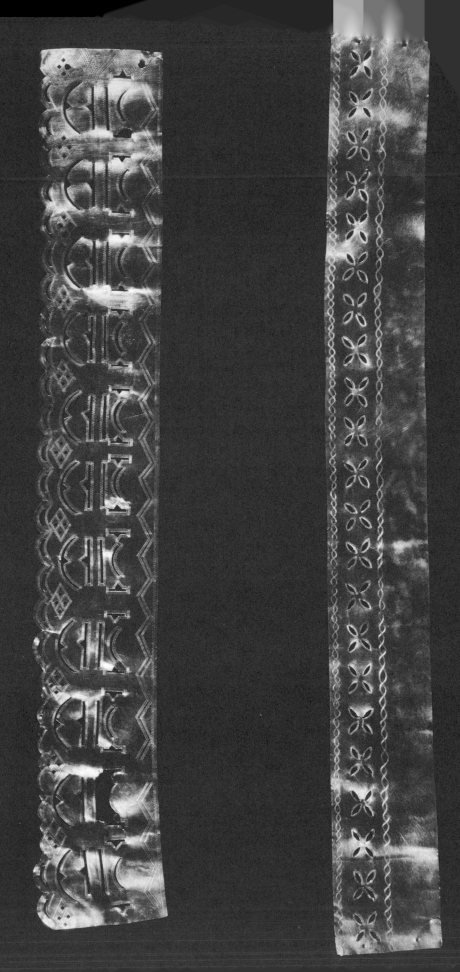

The Metal

Silver has played an unusual role in the civilization of many lands for centuries. Because silver is a precious metal, its role in the eighteenth century was significantly different from that of other metals.

Throughout the sixteenth, seventeenth, and eighteenth centuries all mines of gold and silver in Europe were royal mines—the property of the king. In areas as small as England and France it was comparatively easy for the royal eye to watch mining activity and for the royal hand to collect his just return. The remote location of prospective mines in the New World encouraged entrepreneurs to try to find deposits of precious metal ore in order to work them for their own interests. There would doubtless be enough customers here to patronize the poacher and the potential for great wealth seemed very sure, if rich deposits were found. Unfortunately, they found little silver or gold here, and were, therefore, forced to turn their energies toward finding and refining less exotic metals such as copper, lead, and iron.

The prestigious position of silver among the other metals doubtless exists because it is considered a precious metal. The uses made of it create an image of wealth and luxury. The lowly American Indian shared this concept, for he made only objects of adornment from it when he was able to find it in a state sufficiently pure for him to work. The affluent colonist had his silver plate, consisting of objects with associations of luxury—porringers, tankards, chalices, spoons, candlesticks, and bowls. The prestige of the church was also enhanced with the possession of chalices, flagons, and patens of silver. But more significant than such uses is the fact that silver was used as a medium of exchange. Coins were

Headbands made by American Indians in the early nineteenth century. Examples of such work are extremely rare. *Courtesy Philadelphia Museum of Art.*

made of it in Greek and Roman times, and its use for money has increased from then until now. As a matter of fact, it is now regarded as so precious that substitutes, such as bronze and nickel, are being used for coins, and silver has gained a higher status than it ever had before.

In reading the history of early North America one is not particularly impressed with the importance of the European search for silver and gold. The zeal for the metal has been lost or hidden behind a façade which emphasizes the desire for owning property, the search for personal and religious freedom, as well as the expedient action of clearing English jails. The zeal also lost its fever pitch early in Virginia, where it was probably the most intense, because a "green gold" called tobacco provided the wealth which the ambitious planter sought in America.

The royal family of England and the prosperous merchants must have had mixed emotions, however, concerning the settling of America, as they witnessed the greatest population migration of all time to the New World. They did know their natural resources were rapidly being depleted; they were importing wood and metals from Scandinavia and Russia. If approval for migration needed any stimulus, certainly it was nurtured with the knowledge of the great wealth Spain was acquiring from her colonies in the Western Hemisphere.

A short résumé of some of the important facts will focus attention on the eventful activities of the time. It is reported that on April 12, 1519, Cortes, under the aegis of Spain, landed at what is now Veracruz, Mexico. Fascinated by stories of the great wealth of the inland cities, he destroyed his ships and pressed onward with a band of about 400 men. He professed only friendliness for Montezuma and his subjects, and he was rewarded with gifts, such as a Spanish helmet filled to its brim with gold dust and a disk of silver as large as a cart wheel. Cortes reciprocated by capturing the emperor and slaughtering his subjects.

The wealth of Mexico at the time of Cortes' invasion staggers the imagination. It is said by Benjamin White in his book, *Silver, Its History and Romance*, that:

> During the reign of King Montezuma the cities [of Mexico]
> abounded in products of the loom, featherwork, drinking vessels
> of gold and silver, collars, bracelets, and earrings of the precious met-
> als, as well as grain, fruits, cacao, and articles for literary use such as
> paper manufactured from the ungainly but useful cactus. The writ-

The battery process of forming a sheet of silver from an ingot. Plate I from *Dictionaire des Sciences*. Diderot, Paris, 1763.

ing then current was in the form of Hieroglyphic painting. Monte-zuma maintained a large army, whose dress consisted of quilted cotton, a useful defense against the arrows of Indian tribes. The great chiefs wore cuirasses overlaid with thin plates of silver or gold. Their heads were protected with silver or wooden helmets surmounted with plumes of waving feathers, producing an effect martial and picturesque.

The palace of the kings comprised a vast pile of buildings. The decorations were gorgeous, the walls were draped with rich hangings and the roof inlaid with cedar and scented woods. A quarter assigned to workers in precious metals was to be found in the market-place, where articles could be purchased for use or ornament. Here were to be found on sale many curious silver toys, fashioned ingeniously in the form of birds, or fishes with movable scales.

Much of this wealth came from the great central plateau of Mexico, which was overlaid with a mass of igneous rocks containing such metals as silver, gold, and copper.

Mexico was ruled by Spain from 1521 until 1821. It was autocratically ruled by five governors, Cortes being the first, and sixty-two viceroys. The agents of the rulers were very adept with divining rods, and in extracting secrets from natives concerning the location of rich deposits of silver. From 1542 until 1832 one region produced silver bullion worth more than 667 million pesos. It is estimated that from 1521 until 1891 the silver produced in Mexico was worth more than 4 billion dollars and, if modern mining methods had been used, the figure might have been doubled.

The preceding figures might lead one to assume that Spain's success in securing wealth from the New World in the sixteenth century was the prologue to England's attempts at colonization, the first successful one occurring at Jamestown in 1607. It should be noted that this project was

Anvils, stakes, swages, hammers, and dies used by the silversmith. Plates X and XIII from *Dictionaire des Sciences*. Diderot, Paris, 1763.

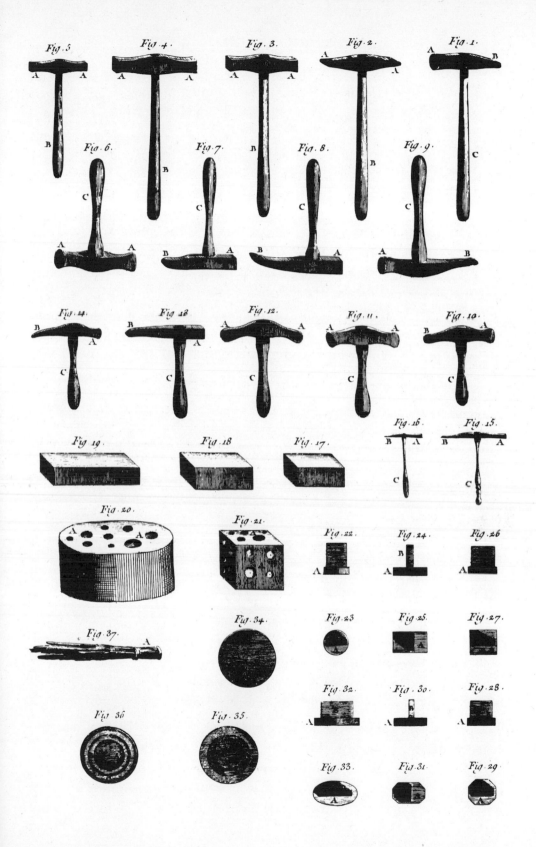

a cooperative venture between the royalty and others who volunteered either their money or their services. And, most significantly, the reasons for colonization enumerated in the charter of the Virginia Company of London were to expand the kingdom, to find a passage to the Orient, and to prospect for precious metals. The only direct feudal relationship with the king was the fact that he was to receive a percentage of the precious metals found.

There is no evidence that provision was made for the mining and refining of precious metals by the first contingent of settlers sent to America; however, the "first supply" which arrived included two goldsmiths, named William Johnson and Richard Belfield. At that time a goldsmith also worked with silver and was equally familiar with both metals. In a letter written to his cousin, John Revoire of Guernsey, Paul Revere, Jr., states that after leaving military service in 1782 he returned to his trade of "Goldsmith" and manufactured fine articles of silverware. Later, a refiner named William Callicut convinced the settlers he had found small deposits of silver and that more could be had for the digging.

Disenchantment concerning the existence of precious metals must have come early in the wake of Virginia colonization, for in 1608 Captain Newport in his report emphasized the richness of the soil and the great quantities of fish, of timber, and of clay for making brick. The possible exports he mentioned included sturgeon, clapboard, wainscot, saxafrage, tobacco, dyes, furs, pitch, resin, turpentine, oils, wine, soap ashes, iron, copper, and pearls, but details regarding the resources of silver and gold were very vague.

Comment by Captain John Smith corroborates Newport's findings, for he says the following about the situation:

> But the worst [of our difficulties] was our guilded refiners with their golden promises made all men their slaves in hope of recompenses: there was no talk, no worke, but to dig gold, wash gold, such a bruit of gold, that one fellow desired to be buried in the sands lest they should by their art make gold of his bones.

The scarcity of gold and silver ores in Virginia is confirmed by the fact that no notices regarding the mining of silver are reported in the *Virginia Gazette* in the eighteenth century. Although foreign intelligence probably had a higher priority as news than local happenings, it is very likely that any activity related to local resources of gold and silver would have been broadcast to the citizens through their important news media.

It is very evident that little silver was found in what is now continental United States in the seventeenth and eighteenth centuries. It should also be noted that the problem of scarcity was compounded by the lack of the metallurgical knowledge required to find and refine silver, a skill which few men must have had at that time.

Silver is obtained by a number of methods. For centuries man knew it existed in nature in a pure form and little knowledge was needed to fashion such metal into small objects of utility and beauty. It has been noted the American Indian made limited use of the metal. Deposits of silver ore usually occur in dry barren areas, such as the southwestern United States, Mexico, Peru, and the arid tablelands of Chile. The ores are known as red silver ore, horn ore, and argentite. Silver is also a by-product of other major mining enterprises, the Anaconda Copper Company being one of the largest producers of silver in America today.

Argentite, a combination of silver and sulphur, is the ore from which silver is most frequently obtained. It is black in color and is often present in areas where native pure silver has been found. It was such black residue from gold workings which led to the discovery of the Comstock lode in Nevada in the late 1850s. The gold workers, being unaware of the value of the substances they were discarding, sold the fringe interest of the mine for a bottle of whiskey, some blankets, a horse, and $2,500 dollars. In the year 1863 silver worth $5 million was dug from the lode, and four years after the deal was made, the mine was valued at $7.6 million.

The appearance of red silver ore also conceals the identity of the valuable metal; a piece containing as much as 60 per cent silver looks to be rusty and worthless. Horn silver is combined with chlorine and is virtually colorless; deposits of this ore have been found in South America.

Silver is also frequently found to be combined with copper or lead. In such cases the major product frequently is not silver, but as a by-product silver is terribly important. One of the unique combinations of silver with other ores is evidenced in the modern discovery of silver at Cobalt, Ontario, Canada. The deposits were first discovered in the late nineteenth century, when the Temiskaming and Northern Ontario Railway was built. As a matter of fact, excavations for the railroad revealed the bed, which has since become one of the most productive silver sources in the world. Deposits vary from native ores in chunks the size of a man to dentritic ore, where veins resemble the trunk and limbs of a tree. Although the major product is silver, the ores contain valuable portions of cobalt, nickel, and arsenic. The Nipissing mine of the region produced from 1904 to 1915 silver valued at $22.1 million.

Despite the fact that prospecting for precious metals in America in the eighteenth century offered little encouragement, the hope for success seems never to have been abandoned. Men experienced in the mining and refining of metals were sent here, many of Germanic origin, because central Europe was the most advanced area in the working of metals. This condition accounts for the presence of so many Germans working in the mines and furnaces of the English colonies.

Only scattered reports are extant about the finding of deposits in America. In 1648 Governor Winthrop, of Massachusetts, reported that the iron works (probably at Saugus, Massachusetts) was going well, and that some silver had been detected in the iron. Thus, at this early date it is evident that men knew silver might become a valuable by-product of other mining operations.

There were rumors of the mining of precious metals in Pennsylvania in the time of the Dutch and Swedish settlements; however, ancient mine holes seem to be the only surviving evidence of such activity there. In 1740 a group of Germans was reputedly operating a copper mine in Duchess County, New York, which also yielded a profitable amount of silver. This facility was abandoned and resumed a number of times, but no deposits were found to warrant continuous operation. About 1750 a shaft 125 feet deep was sunk near New Milford, Connecticut, for the extraction of ore with a content of silver and gold. A German goldsmith is thought to have secretly carried on some silver smelting operations there, but the search for silver was abandoned in favor of the development of ores producing native steel.

It is evident that the only area on the eastern seaboard where sizeable amounts of precious metals were produced was in North Carolina. The so-called "Appalachian Gold Field" crosses the western part of that state. More comment is made about the gold found in the region than silver; however, since both metals are frequently found together, it is likely that some silver was found there. Thomas Jefferson knew about the deposits, and in 1799 a lump of gold was found which is said to have yielded twenty-five pounds of gold twenty-three carats fine (pure gold is 24 carats fine). The Gold Hill Mines of Rowan County (North Carolina) produced a quantity of gold and the Washington Silver mine in the same state produced not only gold and silver, but also iron and lead. Despite all this fragmentary activity, it must be unfortunately concluded that virtually no silver bullion from native ore was available to American silversmiths in the seventeenth and eighteenth centuries. No substantial sources of silver were available until the important discoveries were made in Nevada in the 1850s.

Writers about American silver are unanimous in their opinion that the metal of the silversmith was obtained by melting down coins or remelting earlier objects which were outdated in style. The ruthless destruction of early masterpieces by American silversmiths is an unfortunate event to record, but the advertisements of the craftsmen prove they were willing partners in this catastrophe. Their need for metal was acute and they had little stake in preserving the pieces made by their predecessors, or by English silversmiths. The pressure to keep pace in America with the latest London fashions was persistent, even after the Revolution.

The remelting of coins can be considered the lesser of the two evils. In most cases they were not American coins, so the loss can be accepted with less discomfort. It can hardly be claimed that the aesthetic importance of coins was comparable to that of such vessels as bowls, tankards, and porringers. It was not their unimportance aesthetically, however, that got them into the melting pot, but the absence of banks to protect a man's wealth in coins. It was very difficult to identify one's coins if they were luckily recovered from a thief, so they were turned into identifiable objects often bearing the imprint of the maker, and sometimes the monogram or cypher of the owner. Of course, both of these marks could be removed; however, the wrought object was easier to identify than coins.

It must be noted here that the melting of coins in the eighteenth century did not give rise to the stamping of words such as "COIN SILVER," "COIN," or "PURE COIN" on objects made in the second quarter of the nineteenth century. Objects bearing such imprints are usually less than .900 fine silver, while the standard for sterling has been .925 fine

for many centuries. The balance of the sterling alloy has been universally copper. The addition of copper improves the quality of silver by giving it a richer color, and improves its durability and workability.

The origin of the word "sterling" is explained in a publication of Handy and Harman, called *The Handy Book for Manufacturers*. Their explanation follows:

The Name "Sterling" Is a Contraction
of the Word "Easterling"

In the 12th century five free towns were banded together in the eastern part of Germany under the name of the Hanseatic League. These towns were free not only to make their own laws, but also to issue their currency. When trading with English merchants they gave their coins in payment for British cattle, sheep, grain, and other products. The British soon learned that these coins, which they referred to as the coins of the Easterlings, were always dependable. It is said that Henry II employed some of these Easterlings to improve and

The Intent of the Frontispiece.

1 St. Dunstan, *The Patron of the* Goldsmiths Company.
2 *The Refining Furnace.*
3 *The Test with Silver refining on it.*
4 *The Fineing Bellows.*
5 *The Man blowing or working them.*
6 *The Test Mould.*
7 *A Wind-hole to melt Silver in without Bellows.*
8 *A pair of Organ Bellows.*
9 *A Man melting or boyling, or nealing Silver at them.*
10 *A Block, with a large Anvil placed thereon.*
11 *Three Men Forging Plate.*
12 *The Fineing and other* Goldsmiths *Tools.*
13 *The Assay Furnice.*
14 *The Assay-Master making Assays.*
15 *His Man putting the Assays into the Fire.*
16 *The Warden marking the Plate on the Anvil.*
17 *His Officer holding the Plate for the Marks.*
18 *Three* Goldsmiths, *small-Workers, at work.*
19 *A* Goldsmiths *Shop furnished with Plate.*
20 *A* Goldsmith *weighing Plate.*

A 2   I Do

Frontispiece and explanation. From *A Touchstone for Gold and Silver Wares*. London, 1677.

standardize the English coinage which had become debased. The standard adopted is probably accounted for by the system of weights used. It was based on 11 troy ounces, 2 pennyweights of fine silver and 18 pennyweights of alloy. The word "alloy" was used to designate the base metal (silver). The original designation Easterling Silver was later abbreviated to "Sterling Silver" and the term has come down through the centuries as representing a mark of high quality.

The same publication confirms the composition of sterling silver by saying that:

> The standard sterling alloy contains 925 parts of silver and 75 parts of copper per thousand when cooled. At a normal rate of casting, the microscope shows both of these constitutents to be present. The alloy is entirely liquid at 1640 degrees F. and solid at 1435 degrees F.

Thus from a strictly technological point of view the metal used by silversmiths to fabricate objects should be called "sterling," for the metal is not pure silver. Because the term "silver" has been used to describe this metal for so long a time, it will continue to be used in its traditional concept in this survey.

After the silversmith had obtained his precious commodity from which his product was to be wrought, he was faced with many problems. The first one was to get the metal into a form from which objects could be made. Most authorities on silversmithing simply say that molten metal was cast into ingots and then hammered into a sheet by a process called "battery." These procedures are succinctly illustrated in Plate I from the *Diderot Encyclopedia*. The same illustration also shows men forming objects of silver on stakes and anvils. Plates X and XIII from the *Diderot Encyclopedia* show various tools used by the silversmith. *See pages 19, 20, and 21.*

An earlier illustration, the frontispiece of *A Touchstone for Gold and Silver Wares* (1677 ed.) shows men assaying the metal; over the furnace is mounted a number of the tools used by the silversmith at that time. On the right edge men are shown beating a plate on an anvil. On the upper part of the illustration is an engraving of St. Dunstan, the Patron of the goldsmiths.

An English authority on silversmithing points out that these procedures were used long after other metals were rolled thin on a rolling mill. Possibly the use of the hammer was continued because it was thought that hammering compacted the molecular structure of the metal better than

Coffee pot by Philip Syng, Jr. This unusually graceful, highly ornamented vessel is an outstanding product of one of America's great silversmiths. *Courtesy Philadelphia Museum of Art. Photograph by A. J. Wyatt, Staff Photographer.*

rolling; furthermore, it was a much cheaper procedure as long as labor costs were low, as they were in England in the eighteenth century.

Obtaining the sheet of metal from which to form his object must have been a tedious task for the silversmith in America; however, this was just one of the technological problems he had to resolve. The polyglot sources of his metals suggest that its fineness was a matter demanding his constant attention.

This problem was held to a minimum if he remelted objects of silver wrought in England, for the English government operated assay offices throughout the country and their control of quality was very good. In addition, the appropriate officers of the guild kept a watchful eye on the products of the members there, and objects made of substandard metal went back into the melting pot or were confiscated. In America there were no guilds to discipline the actions of the silversmiths, and only one assay office was briefly operated in Baltimore—from 1814 until 1820.

There are conflicting opinions concerning the fineness of silver used by American silversmiths. Tests made by one party made it very evident that the sterling standard was maintained in the quality of metal used. On the other hand, tests for the alloy have been made as a part of the Andelot-Copeland Museum Science Project, a cooperative program between the Henry Francis du Pont Winterthur Museum and the University of Delaware. Samples from five American spoons were sent to Ledoux & Company at Teaneck, New Jersey, for spectrographic analysis. The results showed that the lowest copper percentage was 10.50 and the highest 14.50 per cent. The copper results were obtained by semi-quantitative X-ray fluorescence. Other similar analyses were made of a larger number of spoons, and the results invariably showed a higher copper content to be present than the sterling standard.

The fact that the sterling standard was not adhered to by all silversmiths is attested by the following advertisement which appeared in *The South Carolina Gazette*, May 2, 1743:

> William Wright is removed into the House where Mr. James Matthews liv'd before the Fire, near Col. Brewton's where he has to sell by retail Barbadoes Rum, Sugar, Molasses, Maderia Wine and Sundry other Goods, at very reasonable rates especially for Ready Money. And whereas 'tis complained that the Silver which is worked up here is not true Sterling Standard, this is to acquaint all Gentlemen and

others, that the said Wright will warrant it to be true Sterling Standard, he will finish his work with the utmost Dispatch. William Wright.

In addition to the problems related to the fineness of his metal, the
silversmith was also plagued with its high cost and the subsequent frugality required in working it. It seems certain that each batch was weighed
when he received his supply, the weight of the object being of such importance that it was frequently recorded on it and, of course, the unused
portion had also to be accounted for. The filings were so valuable that a
leather apron was stretched from the craftsman to the workbench to
prevent their falling to the floor and to easily effect their recovery in a
jar or other container.

But the most demanding facet of silversmithing was the craftsman's
need for an understanding of design and the various ways available to
achieve a desired result. He constantly had to compete with the latest
mode from London, not to mention the fastidious personal tastes of his
patrons. His patronage lay almost completely between rich people and
the church, both of whom were not likely to accept a second-class product and had the discrimination to know when they were getting it.

If any craftsman required the full seven years of apprenticeship to
learn the required techniques of working a medium, as well as sundry
other abilities such as skillful designing, business acumen, and finding
a market for his product, it was the silversmith.

Before embarking on an explanation of the various technological techniques of his work, it should be understood that all products made of
silver (and gold) were called plate. This term applied equally to hollow
ware and flatware. A research into the etymology of the word "plate"
has not brought to light any definite logic in the application of the term
to the objects involved. It is intimated by some writers that the word
evolved very early when only flat objects were made, particularly plates,
and thus the word was indiscriminately used by later generations in
describing all objects made of silver and gold. Dictionaries of the eighteenth century do not include the word in this context. One of the few
definitions found appears in *Zell's Popular Encyclopedia*, 1871, which
is as follows:

> Plate, n [Fr. *plat*; Ger. *platte*; from the Greek, *platys*, broad, flat].
> A flat or extended piece of metal.—Armor, composed of flat, broad
> pieces of metal.—Gold and silver wrought into various articles of

household furniture.—A shallow, flattish dish or vessel from which provisions are eaten at table.

This term must not be confused with the procedure of plating metal, which means that an outer layer of metal is applied to change the appearance and character of certain base metals. Although electricity is used in this process today, objects were "silvered" long before the use of electricity, particularly surfaces on the faces of surveyors' compasses.

The Workshop

There is no doubt that the nature and location of the workshop of the silversmith changed over the years from the time the first craftsman worked here until 1800. The early economy of limited resources doubtless often resulted in the workshop being located within the dwelling of the craftsman as had been done in Europe in earlier times. Possibly the next step was to build the shop near the house, as James Geddy did in Williamsburg, Virginia. That his residence was the more important of the two is attested by the fact that it was built on the corner of Duke of Gloucester Street and the Palace Green, with his shop located next to the house on Duke of Gloucester Street.

By the end of the century embryonic zoning practices were appearing; for example, a silversmith in Philadelphia might have had his shop located on Market Street, while his home was in Germantown. The concentration of shops in a particular area of the city made it convenient for the shopper; he could make his purchases in one area, rather than scurry around to different parts of the city.

Reconstructed and restored shops in Williamsburg carry out the plan that the front portion was devoted to exhibition and sales. A prospective buyer could easily view the ware through a large mullioned window, or easily step in off the street after he decided to make a purchase. Shops were not as efficiently arranged then as factories are today; however, forges when present were placed behind partitions, thus confining the smoke and dirt to one area so that the workers could polish or engrave in well-lighted and pleasant surroundings.

Possibly the most interesting surviving artifacts from the shops of early craftsmen are the attractive signs which hung on a bracket, or were otherwise supported, in the front of the shops. These signs were usually in the form of one of the products of the craftsmen: cordwainers were

View of the residence of James Geddy, a silversmith working in Williamsburg, Virginia, in the third quarter of the eighteenth century. Geddy is thought to have practiced his craft in his home and rented the east shop to merchants or other craftsmen. The floor plan of the house, as well as the exterior appearance, indicates that Geddy was a successful businessman. A costumed hostess stands in the doorway of the Geddy residence.

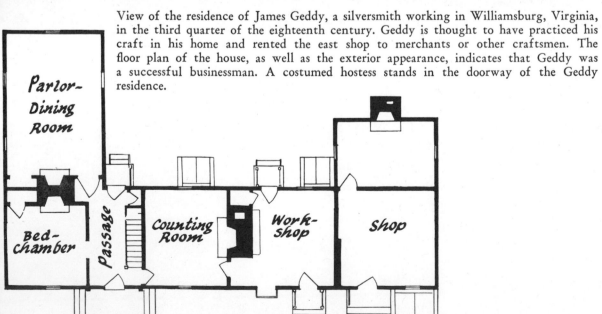

Parlor-Dining Room

Bed-Chamber

Passage

Counting Room

Work-shop

Shop

identified by shoes, tailors by scissors, and silversmiths by objects pertinent to their trade. For example, Isaiah Wagster, a goldsmith and jeweler in Baltimore, Maryland, identified his business as being "At the Sign of the Crown and Pearl." Such signs are highly prized today because of their decorative value; however, it should be noted that the major reason for depicting the craftsman's product in his sign was to accommodate prospective buyers who were unable to read.

It is also very significant to know that many silversmiths practiced allied trades along with their major one of fabricating objects of silver. These sidelines were influenced somewhat by the locality in which the business was operated. Craftsmen doing business in a large city were apt also to be merchants, often selling imported goods along with their own products. The advertisement of Thomas Yon in *The South Carolina Gazette*, August 27, 1763, points out that:

> THOMAS YON, At the sign of the Golden Cup in Beef Market Square, has just imported in the Friendship, Capt. Ball, from London: A neat assortment of jewellry, an eight day clock, and a silver mounted gun: which he will sell for ready cash on a small advance The silversmith's business is carried on by him as usual, and he con-

The sign of James Geddy with the initials "I.G." inscribed on a two-handled loving cup. The crisp lines of the architectural details are evidence of a substantial building and a successful craftsman. Unfortunately, the cup does not photograph well because it is the color of silver, so it does not stand out sharply as it does when viewed from the street.

tinues cleaning and polishing old plate, the same as new. Ladies and gentlemen that employ him, may depend on his utmost diligence in executing their commands, and he hopes for a continuance of their favors.

Less logical pursuits are found among the business activities of other silversmiths, particularly if they worked in rural areas which were not populous enough to keep a craftsman busy making tankards, mugs, or mourning rings. An interesting advertisement of Peter Getz, a silversmith working in Lancaster, Pennsylvania, appeared in *The Pennsylvania Herald and York General Advertiser*, Wednesday, April 28, 1790, telling that, "He also furnishes artificial Teeth, perfectly resembling the real, without inconvenience to the party." His death notice in the *Lancaster Journal*, January 6, 1810, reads as follows: "Died, In this borough, on Friday evening the 29th ult. after an illness of two days, in the 47th year of his age, Mr. Peter Getz, the original improver of the new printing-press, constructed with rollers in lieu of a screw. He was famous for his ingenuity." *See page 13.*

Drawings illustrating observations about the architectural details found in American silver. A knowledge of such details was essential to the success of any silversmith. *See page 44. Courtesy Metropolitan Museum of Art, New York.*

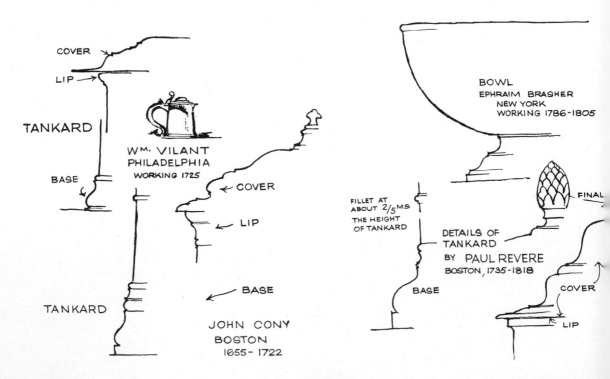

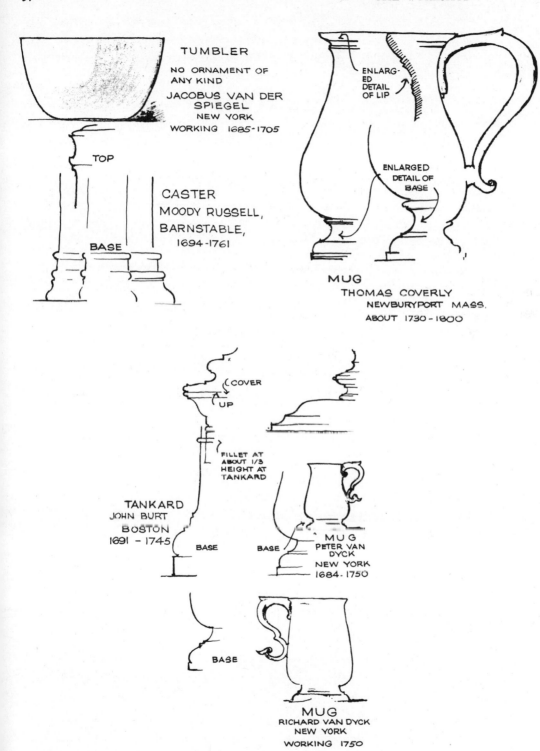

TUMBLER

NO ORNAMENT OF
ANY KIND

JACOBUS VAN DER
SPIEGEL
NEW YORK
WORKING 1685-1705

ENLARG-
ED
DETAIL
OF LIP

ENLARGED
DETAIL OF
BASE

TOP

CASTER
MOODY RUSSELL,
BARNSTABLE,
1694-1761

BASE

MUG
THOMAS COVERLY
NEWBURYPORT MASS.
ABOUT 1730-1800

COVER
UP

FILLET AT
ABOUT 1/3
HEIGHT AT
TANKARD

TANKARD
JOHN BURT
BOSTON
1691 – 1745

BASE

BASE

MUG
PETER VAN
DYCK
NEW YORK
1684-1750

BASE

MUG
RICHARD VAN DYCK
NEW YORK
WORKING 1750

PETER GETZ,

JEWELLER AND GOLDSMITH,
Opposite Mr. Slough's Tavern, in Lancaster ;

BEGS leave to return thanks to his friends and the
public, for the encouragement he has met with since
his commencement in business ; in consequence of which,
he is enabled to pursue it on a more extensive plan, and
on such terms as will secure general approbation.

Said GETZ, continues to make every kind of silver
plate, in the newest fashion. Lockets, Mourning Rings,
Shoe and Knee Buckles, Garnet Rings, Locket Buttons,
Watch Cases, Chains, Seals and Keys, and every kind of
large and small work in gold and silver.

He also performs Engraving with equal assiduity and
elegance. From the experience he has had in these different banches, hopes to merit the favor of an approv-
ing community.

He also furnishes artificial Teeth, perfectly resembling
the real, without inconvenience to the party.

Having lately formed a partnership with

DAVID AIRD,

WATCH-MAKER,
From EDINBURG,

THEY propose carrying on said business in as extensive a manner as possible. Repeating, Horizontal and
Plain Watches made on the most modern construction,
and first quality, and every branch in this business executed with care and attention.

Watches repaired by him, warranted to go well.

Borough of Lancaster, April 19, 1790.

From *The Pennsylvania Herald and York General Advertiser*, April 28, 1790.

Although Mr. Getz was inventive and a fine craftsman to boot, his trades were outnumbered by those of John Inch, who advertised as follows in the *Maryland Gazette*, March 11, 1762.

JOHN INCH, SILVERSMITH

Hereby gives notice, That he still carries on his Silversmith's and jeweller's Business, buys gold and silver, and keeps Tavern as formerly, and has provided himself with a good house painter and glazier lately from London who shall work for any person very reasonably. He also keeps good passage-boats, and has not of his own and others, Vessels fit to carry grain etc. to and from any part of Chesapeake-Bay; he has also for sale a convict-servant Woman's Time. Lately imported, who is a good Stay-maker; a great quantity of Oakum, ship breadth, Delph and Stone ware of divers sorts, too tedious to mention.

The products of all craftsmen reflect various social or economic practices of the era in which they worked. Some of the most curious products of silversmiths and goldsmiths of the eighteenth century were objects related to mourning. One would naturally expect a silversmith to make mourning rings, but one of the unique products was "works in hair." Hair was manipulated into a variety of designs and was often seen mounted in silver, which, of course, explains why the silversmith worked in this unusual medium. An advertisement of G. Smithson in *The South Carolina Gazette*, April 3, 1775, includes a number of unusual items, but particularly focuses attention on his work with hair.

> SMITHSON, G.   (Goldsmith)
> G. Smithson,
>   Returns his most grateful Thanks to his friends for their encouragement, and begs to inform them that he has removed from King-street, to the house late Greenwood and Walker's opposite Mr. Beale's warf, on the Bay; where he humbly solicits the continuance of their Favors. He makes all kinds of Jewellers and Goldsmiths Work, Swords, Cutteaux, Spoons, Buckles, etc. as reasonable as can be imported. Likewise works Hair in Platts, or other curious Forms, such as Landscapes, Flowers, Figures of all kinds, Mottos, Posies, or emblematical Devices, without any assistance from Coulers; engraves Coats of Arms, Crests or Cyphers on Seals or Plates; also Copperplates for Shop-bills, etc. Mourning and Wedding rings on the shortest notice.

Another important facet of the work of the silversmith was repair work. It is very evident that metal was in short supply in America, and a twisted spoon or a broken fork could be more easily repaired than made anew. Furthermore, the frugality of most of the colonists induced them to try repairing before an order for a new object was placed. An advertisement of James Rutherford supports the hypothesis that repair work constituted an important part of the trade. The following advertisement appeared in *The South Carolina Gazette*, November 18, 1751.

> James Rutherford, a regular bred gold and silversmith, just arrived from Edinburg, makes and mends all kinds of plate, and other work in his business, after the best and newest fashions, on reasonable terms. He likewise works in Jewelry, and clasps broken China in the neatest manner, which is work never done here before. His shop is at Mr. William Bisset's, Tayler, in Church-street, next door to Mr. Manigault's.

The wide range of work done by these craftsmen suggests that their shops must have been interesting places, and the number and type of their tools limitless. Inventories of the tools used by several craftsmen are preserved, one of the most extensive being that of Richard Conyers, a London-trained gold and silversmith, who migrated to Boston in the late seventeenth century. The inventory was made by two silversmiths, Jeremiah Dummer and Edward Webb, on April 4, 1709. It might be safely assumed that most craftsmen of the eighteenth century used similar tools, for the technology of the craft changed very little throughout the eighteenth century in America. The value of the tools was attached to each item in the inventory, but because there is little relevance today between the nature of the tool and its value, this information will be omitted from the listing.

1 Large forging anvil	5 Anvils
9 Raising anvils	2 Ditto
1 Large planishing Teast	4 Small Teasts and Swages
1 Spoon Teast	6 Spoon punches & 4 weights
4 Spoon Punches	17 Cutting punches
7 Stakes	27 Dapping punches
1 Skillet & Ingott	1 pr Large stock sheers
Old files 4 lb	3 pr hand sheers
2 Gravers	12 Forging hammers
1 Cutting chisel	25 Small hammers
1 Nurling iron	10 Cornellions 1 Chrystall
3 Old brass pans	10 Glass necklaces
2 Copper pans	5 Ivory boxes
Old Brass patterns	Enamell
1 Large Vise	A parcel Small pearl
3 Forging hammers	Large pearle
25 Small hammers	1 pr Large holding tongs
1 Ring swage	1 Iron
1 Clasp stamp	1 pr Flasks
1 Tankard swage	1 Glew pott
12 Cutting punches	1 pr Hand Bellows
6 Dapping punches	2 Boxes chassing punches
1 pr Flasks	15 Canes
3 pr Sheers	15 Sword blades
4 pr Handvises	1 Glass case
5 pr Plyers	1 Large raising anvil
2 pr Nealing tongs	1 Large skillett
1 pr Casting tongs	9 Rings with Stones and pearls
1 Drawing bench	3 Ditto with large stones
1 pr Large bellows	1 pr Gold earrings
1 pr Hand bellows	Pearl drops

1 pr screw plates	1 Large stone ring
2 Engines for swages	1 pr Stone earrings Sett in silver
3 pr Compasses	1 Gold ring with Six Small stones
2 Iron Triblits	2 pr Stone buckles
3 Drawing irons	2 Stone girdle buckles
1 Nurling iron	1 Olde hatt buckle
1 Pestle 1 Ingot 1 Ladle	6 pr Stone buttons
1 pr Small screw plates	3 pr Ditto
1 Small ingott	—pearle
1 pr Board Vise	1 Lead Stone
3 pr scales	2 Bone heads for canes
3 pr Brass weights	4 Ditto
1 pile Weights	1 Knife handle
1 Sett of Small weights	1 Watch
1 Button stamp	1 Silver tankard and Tobacco box
9 training Weights	Seventy-seven Ounces of Silver in
Glass case	Sundry old & New things in the
2 Burnishing stones	hands of Thomas Milner at /8
Old cast brass	per oz.
3 Bell weights	4 Chrystalls for Watches
1 Pile old weights	

The function of all the tools mentioned in the inventory cannot be definitely established today; however, some reasonably sound conclusions can be drawn from the terminology used. The "skillet and ingott" entry suggests that molten metal was poured into a skillet of cast iron, which subsequently shaped the metal into a disk suitable for the forming of round objects, after it was beaten to the desired thickness. The bellows were used to fan the fire in a forge filled with charcoal.

A variety of shears were available for cutting metal, the largest pair being mounted in a tree stump or on a bench top, where great pressure could be exerted on them with both hands and, if necessary, the weight of the body. Tongs were obviously used to handle hot metal, particularly in the "nealing," or annealing process. The flasks indicate that objects were cast in sand; as for the other tools, such as swages, stamps, chisels, files, plyers, and a glue pot, their function has not changed through the years.

A close scrutiny of the foregoing list inevitably leads to the conclusion that the basic tools of the silversmith were hammers, punches, anvils, and shears. Although the blacksmith has been regarded as king of the hammer-men, the fact that Conyers owned sixty-five of these tools would confirm that he also was in the running. An inventory of the tools of John Burt (1693-1745/46), another Boston silversmith, taken March 20, 1745/46 contains forty hammers. Most of the hammers look very much alike to the untrained eye, but subtle nuances between many of them were quite significant to trained craftsmen. Each silversmith had his favorite tools for doing specific jobs and the loss of one was regarded as a catastrophe. Some of the tools, of course, were made by the silversmith and these would naturally be among his favorites. It is also likely that apprentices were taught to make tools in order to increase their regard for them and to teach them the processes involved, in case they ever needed to make their own. The large number of tools in inventories might be explained by the fact that many of the journeymen employed apprentices who had no tools of their own and, therefore, the tools had to be supplied by their masters.

The large number and variety of hammers is a fascinating aspect of the craft, but, more importantly, one must be aware of the care taken of these tools. All the stakes and hammers had to be kept at a mirror-bright finish for the craftsman to work efficiently. The slightest flaw on the surface of a hammer would be transferred to the surface of the metal with each hammer-blow, and thus the surface of the precious metal would be impaired. Perfection was particularly important on the face of the planishing hammer, for it was the last one to touch the surface of the metal. When hammers and stakes were not in daily use, they were covered with tallow to prevent deterioration. If rusting or flaws did occur on the surface, they had to be eradicated and the tools refinished before being used again.

Despite the fact that fastidious care was taken of the tools, they had to be repaired then as they must be now. An advertisement of Samuel Bissel in the *Boston Gazette*, March 4, 1717, indicates that he "was lately come from England." He also mentions that he was making "all sorts of Blacksmith's and Goldsmith's anvils, Brick irons and stakes," as well as putting "new faces" on old ones at his shop at Newport, Rhode Island. Thus, the painstaking thriftiness of the craftsman is apparent in the way he used his tools, just as it is in his salvaging scraps of silver.

Despite the importance of the heat of the forge, the polish of the hammers and anvils, and the quality of the metal, the most essential factor in silversmithing was the training of the apprentice. It should be noted at the very beginning of this facet of the discussion that, although all the master craftsmen wanted "smart" apprentices, the silversmith emphasized this quality more than other craftsmen. There certainly must have been a hierarchy among tradesmen and the silver and goldsmith must have been at the very top.

Registered for Mr. Charles LeRoux the 23rd day of July Anno Dom. 1719. This Indenture Wittnesseth that Jacob TenEyck aged about fifteen years hath put himself and by these Presents doth Voluntarily and of his own free Will and Accord by and with the Concent of Coenraet TenEyck his father put himself apprentice to Charles LeRoux of the City of New York Goldsmith with him to live and (after the Manner of an Apprentice) to serve from the fifteenth day of July Anno Dom. One thousand seven hundred and Nineteen till the full Term of seven years be Compleat and Ended. During all which Term the said Apprentice his said Master Charles LeRoux faithfully shall serve his Secretts keep his lawfull Commands gladly Every where Obey: he shall do no damage to his said Master nor see to be done by Others without letting or giving Notice to his Master, he shall not waste his Masters Goods nor lend them unlawfully to any, he shall not Commit Fornication nor Contract Matrimony within the said Term, at Cards Dice or any Other unlawfull Game he shall not play whereby his Master may have damage, with his own Goods nor the Goods of others during the said Term without Lycense from his said Master he shall neither buy not sell, he shall not absent himself day nor night from his Masters Service without his leave nor haunt Alehouses Taverns or Playhouses but in all things as a faithful Apprentice he shall behave himself toward his Master and all his during the said Term. and the said Master during the said Term shall by the best Means or Method that he can Teach or Cause the said Apprentice to be taught the Art or Mystery of a Goldsmith. shall find or provide unto the said Apprentice sufficient Meat Drink and Washing in winter time fitting for an Apprentice and his said father to find him Apparell Lodging and washing in summer time and his said Master to suffer his said Apprentice to go to the winter Evening School at the Charge of his father. for the true performance of all and Every the said Covenants and Agreements Either of the said parties bind themselves unto the Other by these presents. In Wittness whereof . . ."

Typical indenture of the eighteenth century. *Courtesy The Museum of Fine Arts, Boston.*

The reasons for this situation are readily apparent. In the first place, the boy had to be scrupulously honest, for he had access to metal of great value, and no master wanted to wake up in the morning and discover that he had been robbed. Since it would have been impossible to identify an ingot of silver in those days, a thief would not have had much difficulty in disposing of such an item. Of equal importance is the fact that the apprentice was working with a metal of great value, and spoilage was certainly frowned upon by the master craftsman. It was possible that an apprentice would work long hours and many days on an object; to discard it and start anew would have been a disastrous procedure.

It might logically be pointed out here that it is almost impossible to find among the products of craftsmen working in the eighteenth century a counterpart of what the twentieth century calls "seconds." Considerable experience by the writer in restoring objects of metal to their original appearance and function has led him to the conclusion that his work was necessary because the utensil had been subjected to ill usage or indiscreet restoration by an incompetent craftsman in the nineteenth century. Thus, the demands on the workmanship of the apprentice were pressing and it is not unlikely that a sizeable number of them were "washed out" before they served their stint and became master craftsmen.

But more importantly, the most demanding facet of the boy's training was an aesthetic insight into the design of the objects he was creating. It is true that many of them were apprenticed to craftsmen who had been trained in England, and thus the taste and sophistication of English products were reproduced in America. But by the end of the eighteenth century the trade was pretty well Americanized, yet a high standard of craftsmanship and design continued to exist in the products of the American silversmith. A quotation from *American Silver of the XVII & XVIII Centuries*, written and illustrated by Cass Gilbert, focuses attention on this very important matter. *See page 36.*

> It was, to me at least, a real discovery to find that in practically all old American and much of the English silver, of what we call the "Colonial Period," the mouldings were replicas or refinements of architectural mouldings of the classic Roman or Renaissance periods.
>
> The Graeco-Roman echinus frequently forms the cup; the fillet and cavetto follow below in classic sequence, as in the tankard by William Vilant of Philadelphia, in the Clearwater Collection, or in the upper moulding of the shaft of the caster by Stephen Emery (1752-1818).

Sometimes the Attic base appears complete with the conge of the column and its fillet, then half-round moulding, fillet, scotia, taurus, and plinth in perfect sequence and proportion as though copied from the base of a Corinthian column. In other pieces there are various combinations of mouldings forming base, cap and cover, all of them of exquisite shape; the cyma recta and the cyma reversa, fillet, bead, ovolo, and cavetto are wrought together with the knowledge and skill of masters of architecture.

These were no uncommon craftsmen . . . nor were they lacking in erudition. They knew their precedent and their proportions and yet knowing worked with free hands, controlled only by the knowledge of their art and impeccable taste.

Because the silversmith made such outstanding products, it becomes evident that he naturally transacted business with a clientele which was an important sector in the society of the period. It might also logically follow that the silversmiths, therefore, became engaged in important matters outside of their daily tasks of hammering, soldering, and polishing.

One example of a craftsman's reaching a position of prestige in his community is that of Joseph Richardson, Sr., of Philadelphia. The following résumé appeared in the *Pennsylvania Journal* after his death on November 22, 1770.

On Saturday morning last died Joseph Richardson, Esq. an eminent Merchant of this city, in the 64th year of his age; a Gentleman whose private virtues, and public spirit justly claimed the friendship, esteem, and confidence of his fellow citizens and others. He served for several years as a representative in the Assembly of this province, with steadyness, integrity and advantage to his country. He filled several other offices of public trust with assiduity and reputation, and devoted a great deal of time to settling disputes and controversies among his neighbors and others; a conduct truly praiseworthy, and for which he deserves the highest encomium. His unexpected death is deeply mourned and lamented by his family and friends, and his loss, as a very useful member of society, regreted by his countrymen, who demonstrated this respect to his memory, by attending his funeral in great numbers to the Quaker's burying ground in this city, where he was interred on Monday.

Thus, esteem for a man's products and for his character seem to coincide, and posterity, sharing this approbation, will be eager to examine the products of such outstanding craftsmen.

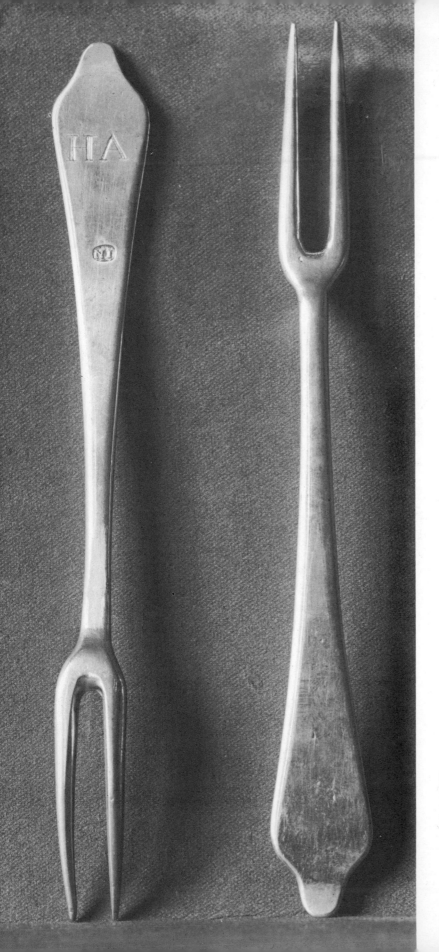

Silver forks made by John Noyes (1674-1749) of Boston. Forks of the type are exceedingly rare. *Courtesy The Museum of Fine Arts, Boston.*

Forks and Spoons

The making of a fork will be the first of the processes used by the silversmith to be scrutinized. Such a procedure might logically be questioned by perceptive readers who know that forks made entirely of silver were very scarce in the eighteenth century. It is reported that forks were invented in Italy and brought to England in the seventeenth century. Despite the fact that they were regarded as objects of luxury in England and America, it is interesting to note that the inventory of silver items owned by Abram de Peyster, who died in New York in 1728, included thirty-seven silver forks. The fact that they were not described as "silver-handled" suggests that they were made completely of silver and were not the silver-handled type which became popular later in the century. The tines of the silver-handled fork were made of steel.

The reason for choosing the fork as the first example of silversmithing lies principally in the fact that silver's most important quality, malleability, was particularly important in the making of this object. Another, and more easily understood, word for malleability is "stretchability." A second reason for its choice lies in the fact that relatively little skill was required to make it.

First, a blank of metal had to be obtained before the stretching procedure could be started. It is not probable that a small piece of silver of the approximate size needed to make a fork was prepared, for the processing of many small pieces would have been wasteful of time and more difficult than the pounding out of a larger piece. When a piece of the desired thickness became available, a small rectangle was removed by sawing, shearing, or cutting with a cold chisel. This blank was undersize for the finished fork, because allowance had to be made for stretching the metal at the desired points. Next, the metal had to be annealed (softened) to relieve the strains incurred in the battery process, commonly known

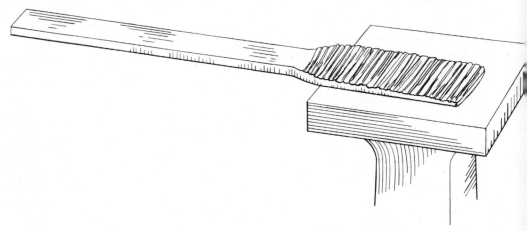

as work-hardening, which inevitably occurs when most metals are hammered.

The actual production of the fork started by placing the broadside of the blank on a silversmith's anvil, known as a stake, and striking it crosswise with the straight end of a cross-peen hammer. This rounded-wedge-shaped hammer, falling with some pressure upon the silver, spread the

metal outward on each side of the spot where the pressure was applied. Repeated blows of the hammer increased the length of the blank and reduced its thickness, at the same time slightly increasing its width.

Next, the handle end of the blank was placed on the stake, and blows applied lengthwise with the wedge end of the hammer. This procedure increased the width to the dimension desired for the handle and also diminished the thickness of the blank.

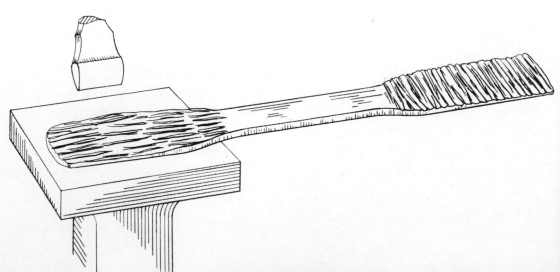

The center portion of the blank was then laid edgewise on a stake and struck with the cross-peen hammer until the desired width and thickness were produced. This operation not only reduced the width of the blank, but also increased the thickness where the handle would otherwise have been very weak. The metal had to be annealed several times during the forming process.

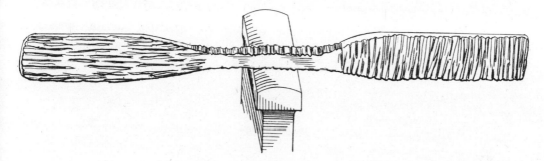

The blank was then thick and thin, wide and narrow at the proper places, but the entire surface was badly distorted from such vigorous pounding. To make the entire blank reasonably smooth, the craftsman used the slightly convex face of a planishing hammer. Each blow partially overlapped another until the entire surface was covered.

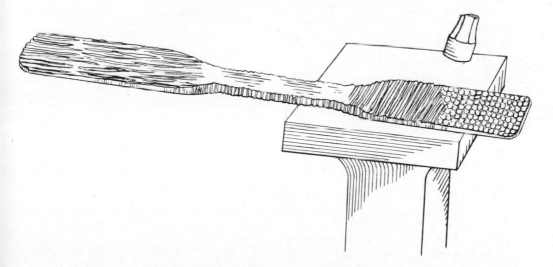

A meticulous craftsman planished his products several times, each time easing the pressure of the blow and more nearly producing an even surface. The shallow facets produced by this technique are often barely visible on old objects of silver, for they were partially removed by the craftsman in the finishing process, as well as by the housewife who polished them hundreds of times throughout a lifetime of use. The marks produced by the planishing process were not the sharp pock marks found on pseudo-reproductions made in the twentieth century.

The final layout of the shape followed. The tines (either two or three) were marked with an awl as was the design on the end of the handle. An effort was made to achieve the final form as nearly as possible with the hammer to avoid wasting any of the precious metal by cutting it away. The final design was achieved by sawing details of the shape which could not be achieved by any other method. Later, edges were made smooth and

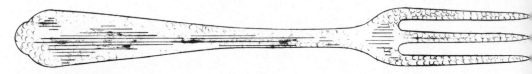

contours refined by using such abrasives as pumice or rottenstone. At this point the blank was smooth, straight, and flat. The desired relationship of the tines with the handle was obtained by a few deft blows with a mallet while the silver was supported on an appropriately shaped stake.

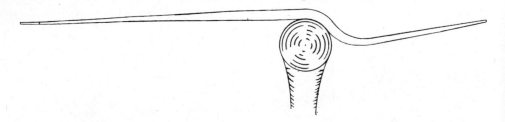

Finally, it should be noted that repeated heating and cooling of the silver created an oxidation of the surface of the metal called fire-scale. The areas of the fork which were filed and polished were bright, so the surface was divided into bright and dark areas. It is likely that the silversmith removed most of the fire-scale before he declared the product ready for the customer.

It has been pointed out that some forks were made entirely of silver and used in the eighteenth century; there is, however, a preponderance of evidence that spoons were much more plentiful. As a matter of fact, historians and antiquarians suggest that they were not only more numerous, but that they were the first objects of importance made by silversmiths in America.

The great number of spoons arises from a variety of circumstances. In the first place, they were small objects and required little metal for their manufacture. They were a major eating utensil, particularly if only one utensil was available. Although not completely satisfactory, they could substitute for either a fork or a knife. It is also evident that it was a symbol of wealth, and the saying that a child was born with a silver spoon in its mouth was probably almost a matter of fact in many cases.

Like the fork, the blank for the spoon was obtained from a larger sheet which had been reduced to the approximate thickness desired. The form, however, was not a perfect rectangle, for the bowl of the spoon required more width than the tines of the fork. Therefore, the blank was a little wider at one end than at the other.

Work could start at either end. To form the blank for the bowl, the metal was placed broadside on a stake and struck lengthwise with the cross-peen end of a hammer until sufficient width was provided. The dotted line on the drawing indicates the shape of the finished bowl. It must be noted, however, that at the narrow portion in the center toward the rear of the projected form of the bowl, the metal was not stretched, but left its full thickness to provide adequate metal for forming the rat-tail on many spoons of the period.

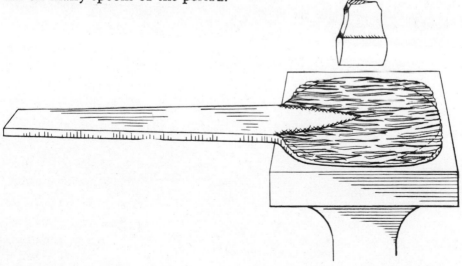

Next, the handle end of the blank was placed on a stake and struck lengthwise, until the desired width was obtained.

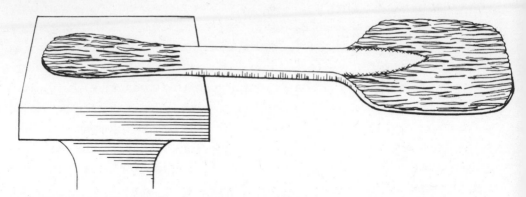

Finally, the center portion of the handle was placed edgewise on a stake and pounded until the desired thickness and width were obtained. Throughout these forming processes the blank had to be annealed several times.

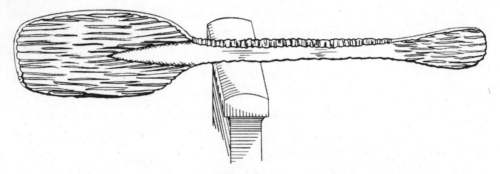

Because the cross-peen end of the hammer distorted the surface of the metal, it was necessary to make the surface reasonably smooth by planishing it, as was done with the fork. The ridge in the center, however,

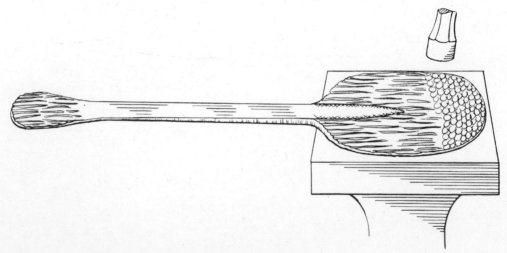

was untouched in this procedure for its full thickness had to be maintained. This heavy part not only made the spoon rigid, but also added to its attractiveness.

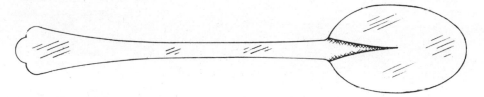

After the layout for the finished shape and size of the spoon was completed, hammering and filing brought it to its final form. Then the flat surface of the bowl was rested on a lump of lead and the bowl made the proper depth with a hollowing hammer. The radius on the face of the hammer coincided as nearly as possible with the finished shape of the bowl, so that no unusual depressions were created which had to be removed. The soft lead allowed the ridge, or rat-tail, on the bottom of the bowl to "seat itself" without distortion while the bowl was hammered into the desired contour.

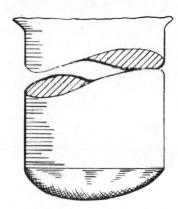

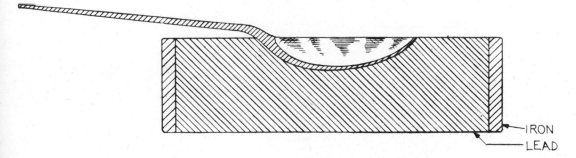

IRON
LEAD

Swage of iron with an eagle engraved in the surface. Has a small terminal tab which overlapped the bowl of the spoon. By laying the blank of silver on the swage, with excess provided for the tab or in some cases the rat-tail, the desired shape could be hammered into the bottom surface of the spoon. *Courtesy Old Salem, Inc., Winston-Salem, North Carolina.*

Some silversmiths had a swage for shaping the rat-tail, before the bowl was shaped. A flat piece of iron had a tapering groove filed into it into which the ridge was pounded to form the rat-tail. Such a device was used in the eighteenth and nineteenth centuries to create a rat-tail, an impression of a shell, or an eagle on the bottom of the bowl. After the desired impressions were made the spoon was then hollowed on the lead.

In the *Diderot Encyclopedia* a swage with male and female parts is shown. With such a tool the rat-tail was simultaneously shaped with the bowl of the spoon. In any of the three methods described irregularities were created on the inner surface of the bowl, which had to be removed by scraping.

The final filing and smoothing were given to the spoon, and the handle bent to its proper relationship with the bowl. The elliptical shape of the

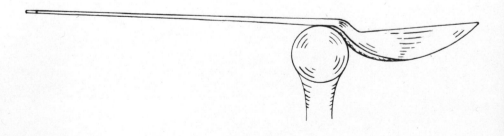

bowl illustrated was widely used in the first half of the eighteenth century. Toward the end of the century the shape of the spoon became narrow at the end opposite the handle, resembling the shape used throughout the nineteenth and into the twentieth century.

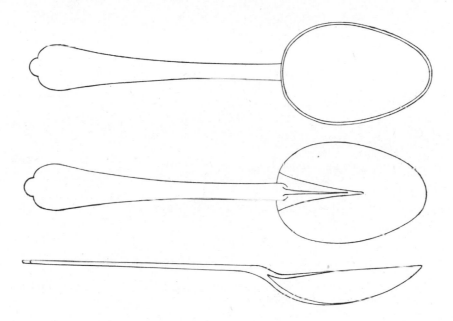

Two spoons by John Burger, New York, late eighteenth century. The shape of these spoons is typical of the period. The handles were quite slender near the bowl, the rat-tail was usually omitted, and the end of the bowl became more pointed. This bowl shape was widely used with the later "fiddle pattern" handle and is much the same shape as a bowl in modern times. *Kauffman collection.*

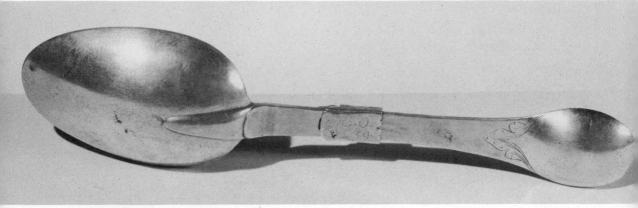

A most unusual example of a folding pocket spoon by Caesar Ghiselin, Philadelphia (1670-1734). The trifid arrangement of initials can be faintly seen on the top of the handle near the hinge. They are probably the initials of the owners. The large initials could be those of a later owner. It is possible that the rat-tail form on this spoon, as on some others, was filed instead of swaged. *Courtesy Philadelphia Museum of Art; photograph by A. J. Wyatt, Staff photographer.*

A description of the production of a spoon, and possibly a fork, would not be complete without some explanation about the name and/or the initials usually found on the handle, rarely on the bowl. The name of the maker was imprinted on the bottom side of the handle with a steel die, which created an intaglio impression on the silver. ("Intaglio" indicates that a depressed cartouche was made with raised letters.) The die was made of steel; however, the shaping and making of the letters was executed while the steel was soft, and the steel later hardened to withstand the frequent pressure applied by striking the top end with a hammer. An imperfect impression of the maker's name can be attributed to the fact that the die was not held evenly when the name was imprinted, or that it could have been obscured at a later time by injudicious polishing.

In the earliest times the silversmith, because of frugality or precedent, used only the initials of his given name and surname in his die. In the eighteenth century he usually used the initial of his given name and his complete surname, and on some occasions used his full name. In the nineteenth century the place of manufacture was often added, particularly

The frugality or, possible better, the ingenuity of the colonial silversmith and his patron is exemplified in these objects combining forks and spoons, called "sucket forks." The word "sucket" is derived from "succade" which, in the fifteenth century, referred to fruit preserved in sugar, either candied or in syrup. The term was also used in describing vegetables which had been similarly treated. *Courtesy The Heritage Collection, Old Deerfield, Massachusetts.*

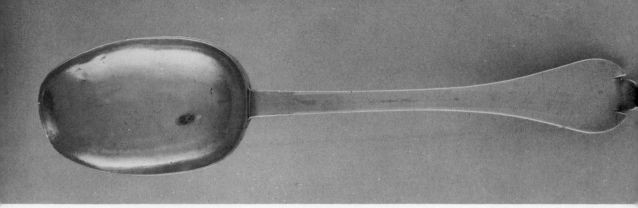

This style of spoon was made in America at the beginning of the eighteenth century. The ovoid shape of the bowl, slightly flattened at each end, was accompanied by a "rat-tail" under the bowl. The width of the stem slowly widening into three lobes at the end was known as a "trifid" end. The sharp indentations at the end of the handle soon were changed into three rounded notches. These are called "wavy-end" handles. *Courtesy Henry Francis du Pont Winterthur Museum.*

if he worked at a prestigious place such as Philadelphia, New York, Boston, or Newport.

Needless to say, the absence of a maker's mark usually deflates the value of an object, unless it can be identified through family ownership, or by recognizing in it the unique style of a particular maker. It might also be noted that some early unmarked pieces have been imprinted in modern times with the names of famous craftsmen. The authenticity of marks can usually be confirmed or denied by experts who have made a comprehensive study of the subject.

L
S ✠ H

Near the end of the handle one often finds initials engraved on the top or bottom. Sometimes three initials appear in a triangular arrangement, the upper one standing for the family name of the groom, while

Intaglio die for marking objects made of silver by J. Vogeler, a silversmith working in early nineteenth century in Salem, North Carolina. *Courtesy Old Salem, Inc. Winston-Salem, North Carolina.*

the bottom two stand for the given names of the bride and groom. A similar arrangement of initials is often found inlaid on pieces of furniture such as clocks or cases of drawers. If the object were a wedding or birth gift, a date was sometimes included.

Although it cannot be said that engraving was absolutely a part of silversmithing, some silversmiths were very competent engravers. They not only engraved a few initials on a spoon, fork, or tankard, but also executed intricate designs, such as coats of arms, on important objects of silver. Advertisements in newspapers often enumerate these various skills of the silversmith, such as the one of Dan Carrel, who advertised in the *Charleston City Gazette and Advertiser*, on April 20, 1790, as follows:

DAN CARREL
Silversmith and Jeweller
At the sign of the Silver Coffee Pot—No. 129 Broad Street, Makes, Sells, and Repairs anything in the above branches. Counting—house-watch seals, coats of arms, and all manner of Engraving on gold, silver, steel, etc., executed in the best manner, and on reasonable terms. . . .

Among some of the well-known silversmiths who were competent engravers was John Coney, who engraved the plates for the first paper money printed in America, and the illustrious Paul Revere, better known as a sentryman than as an engraver. An advertisement in the *Boston Gazette*, February 4, 1765, focuses attention on the fact that Revere not only engraved his silver products, but also copper plates for printing.

Spoon by John Vogeler. The imprint of an eagle was made from the swage block with two eagle impressions on it. *See page 54. Courtesy Old Salem, Inc., Winston-Salem, North Carolina.*

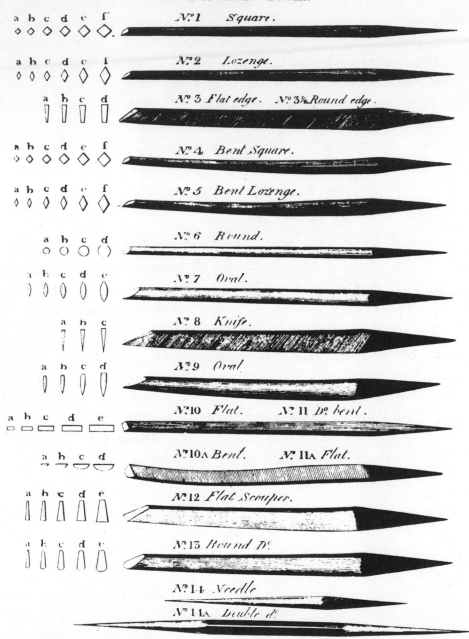

ENGRAVER'S TOOLS

Nº 1 *Square.*

Nº 2 *Lozenge.*

Nº 3 *Flat edge.* Nº 3½ *Round edge.*

Nº 4 *Bent Square.*

Nº 5 *Bent Lozenge.*

Nº 6 *Round.*

Nº 7 *Oval.*

Nº 8 *Knife.*

Nº 9 *Oval.*

Nº 10 *Flat.* Nº 11 *Dº bent.*

Nº 10A *Bent.* Nº 11A *Flat.*

Nº 12 *Flat Scouper.*

Nº 13 *Round Dº*

Nº 14 *Needle*

Nº 14A *Double dº*

Typical shapes of engraving tools used by a silversmith in the eighteenth century (and in the twentieth). When new, they were two to three inches long, excluding the handle; however, they were frequently made shorter by deliberately breaking them or because of frequent sharpenings. From *Key to the Manufactories of Sheffield* by Jos. Smith, 1816. *Courtesy Sheffield City Libraries.*

SCRAPERS &c

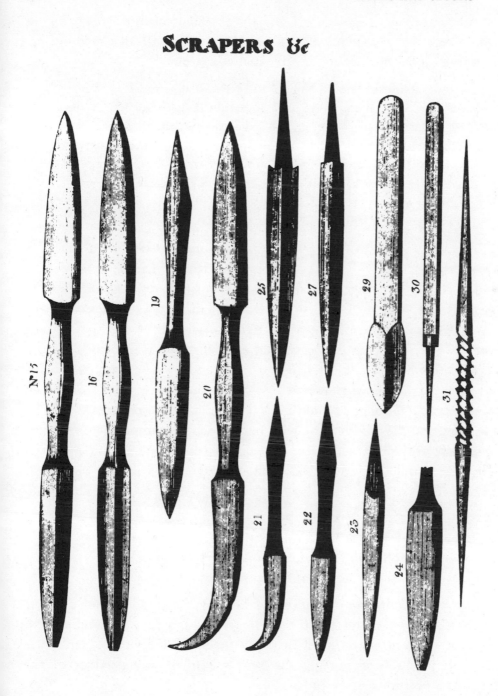

Scrapers used by engravers to remove unwanted irregularities from the surface of the metal being engraved. From *Key to Manufactories of Sheffield* by Jos. Smith, 1816. *Courtesy Sheffield City Libraries.*

The advertisement is an unusual one for the eighteenth century, for, in fact, it describes a product of the combined efforts of two men, an incident which did not occur very often at that time.

> Just published. And to be Sold by Josiah Flagg, and Paul Revere, in Fifth Street, at the north end of Boston, a collection of the best Psalm-tunes, in two, three, and four Parts, from the most celebrated Authors; fitted to all Measures, and approved by the best Masters in Boston, New England. To which are added, Some Hymns and Anthems; the greater part of them never before Printed in America.
>
> Set in Score by   Josiah Flagg
> Engraved by   Paul Revere

The art (or craft) of engraving was executed by holding a short V-shaped tool (called a graver) with a small stubby handle between the thumb and the forefinger, the other fingers steadying the position of the tool as it removed small slivers of metal from the surface. A steady and controlled application of pressure was essential, for if the tool slipped from its intended course, the surface of the metal was marred with a deep scratch. Such scratches had to be repaired by a scraper, which removed metal adjoining the scratch, or by a burnisher, which smoothed the surface by rubbing adjoining metal back into the scratch.

Finally, for the silversmiths who never became competent engravers, there were craftsmen who were exclusively engravers. Such a man was John Sacheverell, who advertised in the *Pennsylvania Gazette*, March 22, 1732, as follows:

JOHN SACHEVERELL
GOLDSMITH
Who performs all sorts of Engraving or Carving in Gold, Silver, Brass, Copper, Steel, after the newest and neatest manner.

It seems evident from a survey of two of the smallest and simplest objects made by the silversmith that his craft was a very demanding one. The best of them were skilled in many facets of their trade, and their surviving products are among the most sought of any product of the eighteenth century.

Plates and Basins

After discussing the making of a fork and spoon of silver, one's attention might logically turn toward the making of another eating utensil, a plate. It is a well-established fact that many early plates were made of wood and of pewter; however, it is somewhat puzzling to discover that few plates were made of silver. As a matter of fact, only one plate is mentioned in *Historic Silver of the Colonies and Its Makers*, by Francis Bigelow, and none is listed in the index of *American Silver of the XVII & XVIII Centuries*, by C. Louise Avery. One plate is illustrated in *American Silver* by John Marshall Phillips, who curiously emphasizes the richly engraved rim of the plate made by John Coney, but neglects to comment about the rarity of plates. The plentiful supply of drinking vessels, ranging from those used for communion to those used in taverns suggests that owners of silver vessels were more interested in drinking than in eating, albeit some of the drinking occurred in the church, not only at communion, but also at funerals.

It is interesting to note that even outside the context of silver objects, the word "plate" is an elusive one. For example, the term does not appear in the Fourteenth Edition of *The Encyclopedia Britannica*, nor can it be found in other common sources of such information. The first definition, however, under the word plate in the *Encyclopedia: or a Dictionary of Arts and Sciences, and Miscellaneous Literature*, printed by T. Dobson, in Philadelphia, 1798, gives the following information:

> PLATE, a term which denotes a piece of wrought silver, such as a shallow vessel off which meat is eaten.

It has been previously pointed out that the word "plate" was widely used in the seventeenth and eighteenth centuries to describe all objects made of silver or gold. In this context most references define the word "plate," but far fewer mention it as a utensil used when eating.

If there were few large ones, there certainly were many small ones called patens. Patens were small plates, usually five to seven inches in diameter, used to serve bread in communion services in England and America. It might be logically concluded that, although the poverty of the colonists did not permit silver plates to be made for eating in the home, the combined resources of a congregation might have permitted such a one to be used in their church. It might also be pointed out that other communion vessels, such as flagons and chalices, were also made of silver.

Because of an erroneous idea developed in modern craft classes about the technique used to form shallow vessels, it seems logical to first dispel the idea that shallow plates were beaten down into a preshaped mold of hard wood, the depression having the desired shape and depth of the product. Although this procedure does enable an embryonic craftsman to produce an object, this technique restricts the depth and diameter of the product unless a very large number of molds is available, and this was not the procedure followed by the silversmiths of the eighteenth century.

The process used in making a plate or a paten was called "sinking." Sinking invariably infers stretching (ductility) but by tension rather than by compression, as was used in the making of the fork and the spoon.

To make a shallow plate the sheet metal was first uniformly reduced to the optimum thickness for the object to be produced. A plate twelve inches in diameter required a thicker piece of metal than a plate six inches in diameter. It will be evident that the metal was slightly thinned in the sinking operation; the reduction of thickness, however, in such a shallow vessel was a negligible consideration.

The work was started by cutting an annealed disk slightly oversize to allow for final trimming. The diameter of the depressed portion was struck from the center with a compass, if round; a template was used for other shapes.

The end-grain of a hard piece of wood, such as maple or birch, was then set upright in a vise. The arc of the outside diameter of the plate was then inscribed on the flat top surface of the block, so that the sinking line coincided with the edge of the block. Two nails were driven into the top surface of the block and, as the disk was rotated against the nails,

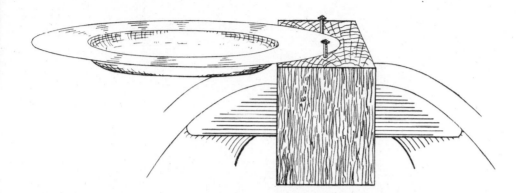

blows at the sinking line created a slight depth, which was increased by repeating the operation until the desired depth was obtained.

After each rotation of the disk the edge, or intersection of the flat rim with the dished part, became rounded a bit. The rim was made flat by

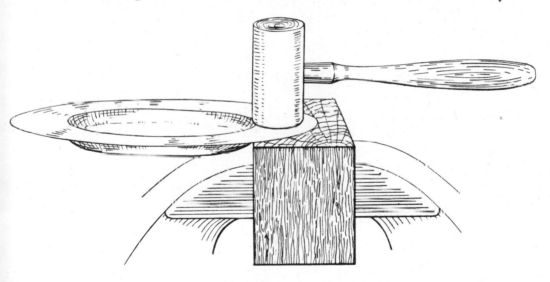

striking it with a hammer or a mallet. This procedure usually created a wavy contour in the edge, which was removed by placing the plate upside down on a flat surface and applying pressure with a block of hard wood and a hammer. After the desired depth was obtained, the bottom had also to be made flat by using a flat-faced mallet or a small block of wood with a hammer. After the shaping was completed and the rim and the bottom of the paten made flat, the uneven booge or bulge had to be

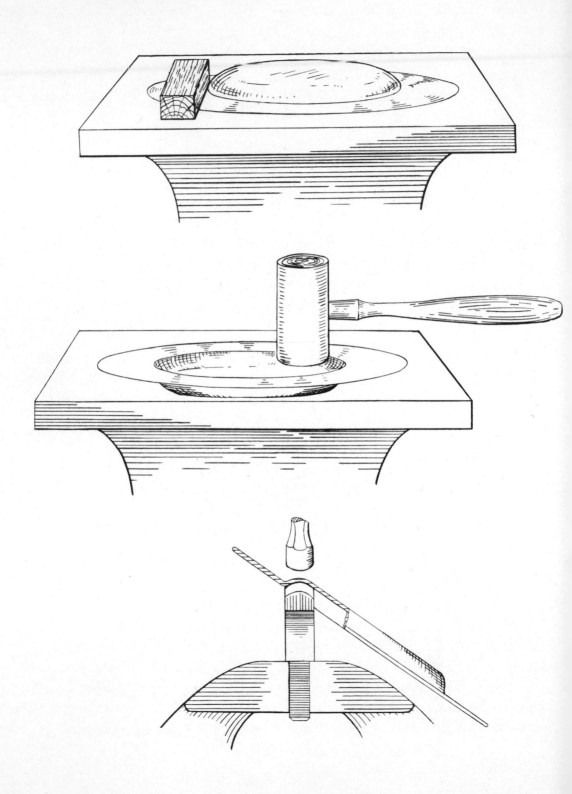

planished to make the metal hard and bring the shape into perfect roundness. This was a difficult operation to perform on such a small area, with
a depth of possibly only a half inch.

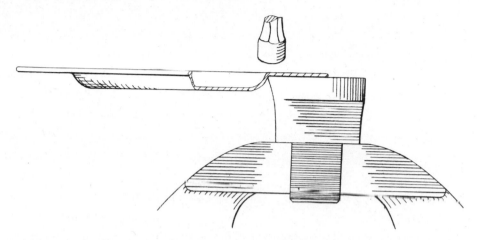

Finally, the flat rim was lightly planished to make it rigid and provide
an even-textured finish found on objects of silver made by hand methods.
The usual trimming and polishing with pumice made it ready for the
customer.

Although the word "basin" and the various uses of the object are not
completely obsolete, it must be admitted that confusion could easily arise
concerning the form and function of the two objects, bowls and basins.
Such confusion is not completely a matter of semantics today for the
Oxford English Dictionary, Oxford, 1933, comments as follows about the
two objects:

> Historically, a *bowl* is distinguished from a *basin* by its more hemi-
> spherical shape; a 'basin' being proportionally shallower and wider, or
> with the margin curved outward, as in the ordinary wash-hand basin;
> but the actual use of the word is capricious, and varies from place to
> place; in particular, the ordinary small earthenware vessels, used for
> porridge, soup, milk, sugar, etc., which are historically bowls are so
> called in Scotland and in U.S., are always called in the south-east of
> England, *Basins.*

The significant point of difference seems to relate to their shape, and
tradition supports the statement that a basin is "shallower and wider"
than a bowl. This difference, combined with the fact that basins often

have a wider brim than a bowl, suggests that a basin is closely related to a plate; at least there were a number of similarities in their making. As a matter of fact, one might almost say that a basin was a hybrid between a plate and a bowl.

The wide brim seems to have been an essential part of the basin made for domestic or baptismal use, for most of them have such a brim. However, one made by Philip Syng as a gift to Christ Church in Philadelphia from Robert Quary has a very narrow brim and really resembles a bowl, as do a few others. They generally range in diameter from ten to fourteen inches, but John Coney made one with a diameter of seventeen inches which is owned by the Second Congregational Church of Marblehead, Massachusetts.

One must assume that there was a logical reason for wide brims because so many had them. They certainly were an aesthetically pleasing feature; they provided an adequate hand-grip when in use, and on many, significant inscriptions were engraved. The Reverend Brattle, who apparently owned one for domestic use, bequeathed it to his church for baptismal use with directions that an appropriate inscription be placed on it. The inscription is, "A Baptismal Basin consecrated, bequeathed, & presented to the Church of Christ in Cambridge, his Dearly beloved Flock, By Revd. Mr. Wm. Brattle Pastr of the Sd Church: Who was translated from his Charge to his Crown, Febr 15: 1716/17."

It was a general rule that, regardless of the technique used to manufacture a vessel, one of great depth required a thicker piece of silver than one that was shallow. If a basin had a flat horizontal brim, the first stage of production was similar to the making of a plate. The diameter of the depressed part was inscribed on the disk, nails were properly placed in a block of wood so that the inscribed line coincided with the edge of the block. By holding the metal firmly against the nails and the flat top of the block, the bulge or booge was started with a sinking hammer. By rotating the disk and striking it with the hammer, a depression similar to that of a plate was soon created. The usual precaution had to be taken to keep the transitional edge sharp and the brim flat.

After the object looked like a plate, the silversmith could obtain the desired depth for his vessel by using one of two methods, or possibly both. He could transfer his object to the tree trunk and by tensional stretch-

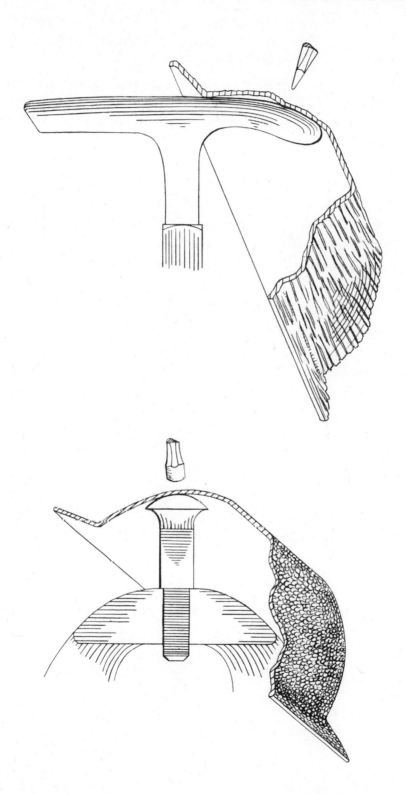

ing make the piece considerably deeper. There were, however, distinct dangers in using this method exclusively, for continued stretching made the metal paper-thin or possibly made a break in it.

The better procedure was to place the basin upside down on a round stake and really raise the metal, as was done in making cups and beakers. This method of stretching by compression permitted an even stretching of the metal, and minimized the hazards of thinness and breakage.

After the desired shape and size were obtained, the distorted surface of the metal had to be made smooth by planishing it. This procedure could be done on the same stake used to stretch and shape the metal. Some basins have a domed center, which is difficult to avoid in the planishing process, and also provides a solid footing on which the basin rests. The usual filing and polishing were the final steps in the making of a basin.

Cups and Beakers

O ther objects made by the silversmith, which appear to fit into the "simple" category, are cups and beakers. Dictionary definitions are very imprecise in distinguishing the characteristics of the two objects; however, it is generally agreed that a cup is a short vessel used for drinking and a beaker is a tall one employed for the same purpose. It might also be noted that while American cups have handles, beakers usually do not.

The earliest method for making these vessels, and the most desirable from the connoisseur's point of view, was to fashion them of one piece of metal, a process called raising. This fundamental and important procedure will subsequently be explained in full detail, for it was by this method that most of the important hollow ware of the eighteenth century was made.

A method used late in the century was to make separate patterns for an object, one for the sides and another for the bottom of the vessel. After these patterns were placed on sheets of silver, the craftsman traced around them, cut the metal to size, shaped the parts, and assembled them by soldering. Objects formed by this method have one vertical joint in the side and a circular one around the perimeter of the bottom. Although the obvious joinery in most pieces fabricated by this method was expertly done, sometimes the joint at the bottom is quite indifferently finished.

To make a cup of one piece of metal the craftsman first had to cut a disk the desired size. This size varied among craftsmen, for each used personally developed techniques, but the differences were slight. Great care was exercised in cutting the metal, since waste had to be held to a minimum.

The raising procedure was begun by laying the disk of metal on the end section of a large tree trunk, which was standard equipment in most

shops. The end grain of the wood had the combined qualities of hardness and resiliency, which permitted the metal to bend or stretch in direct relation to the pressure applied to it with a hammer or a mallet. After many years of use, hollows of different diameters and depths developed in the wood, and the silversmith could choose the one best suited for his immediate need. Because of their great weight, the sections of wood were not attached to the floor, and they were probably lower than bench height, so that the craftsman could sit on a low stool while he worked.

By using a hollowing hammer, one with a radius larger than that of a sinking hammer, the craftsman struck the disk in a series of concentric circles, starting at the outer edge and working inward toward the edge of the bottom, or vice versa. This procedure is known as tensional stretching. In this way a form was created with a flat bottom and flaring sides. Although considerable depth could be obtained by this method, it had only limited use for to obtain great depth the metal would be stretched too thin, and the large diameter of the disk could *not* be reduced to the small diameter of the top of the cup. Thus, to make the sides perpendicular to the bottom another technique had to be employed. Hammer blows were applied to the outside of the disk instead of to the inside, as was originally done. This was *raising*.

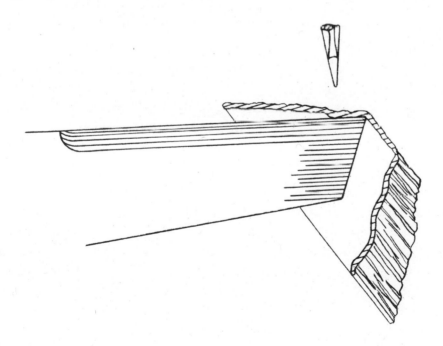

It must be quite evident that to create a shallow bowl from a disk of metal was a relatively easy task, for little shaping had to be done and, therefore, a modicum of skill was required to execute such work. As the contour of the piece changed from the horizontal to vertical, the degree of skill required increased in direct ratio to the work involved. If the diameter of the neck of an object were smaller in diameter than the sides, the problem of raising increased proportionately. A cup appears to be a simple object to make, and by comparison to many others it was; however, it is likely that apprentices practiced the raising technique with a piece of copper many times before they were allowed to work with silver. The working properties of copper are similar to those of silver, and in case of failure in initial trials, the loss of copper would be much less costly than that of silver.

To start the raising process the partially shaped disk was supported on a stake in an inverted position so that it could be struck on the outside. The very slightly rounded end of the stake supported the disk at the point where the raising procedure was to begin. By striking the metal with a raising hammer slightly in advance of the point on which it was supported, the metal was slowly contracted, the diameter reduced, and the sides raised. A skillful craftsman could raise the sides from a horizontal to a vertical position in about three or four "passes" over the outer surface of the metal.

Certain problems were encountered in the raising process. The object had to be kept perfectly round, an even thickness had to be maintained at all points and, when finished, the top had to be level.

The top edge could be kept reasonably level by careful workmanship and by striking any high point which developed with the hammer. This process was called "upsetting" in blacksmithing, but in silversmithing it was called "caulking." Sometimes caulking was deliberately done to increase the thickness of the metal at the top edge, thus making it more rigid and attractive. A certain amount of filing could also be done; however, this was a wasteful procedure and frowned upon by good craftsmen. The ridges created in the sides of the cup could be kept to a minimum by careful workmanship, thereby reducing the time required for planishing to make the surface smooth.

Regardless of the skill of the silversmith in the raising process, the sides had to be completely planished, and the bottom made smooth and flat on a bottoming stake. The angle between the sides and the bottom had to be carefully squared, but not hammered to force a slit in the metal or make it unusually thin at the point of intersection.

The bottom edge of the cup was often decorated by attaching an ornamented band of silver. This procedure also slightly increased the diameter of the base and made the object appear more stable. The band of silver

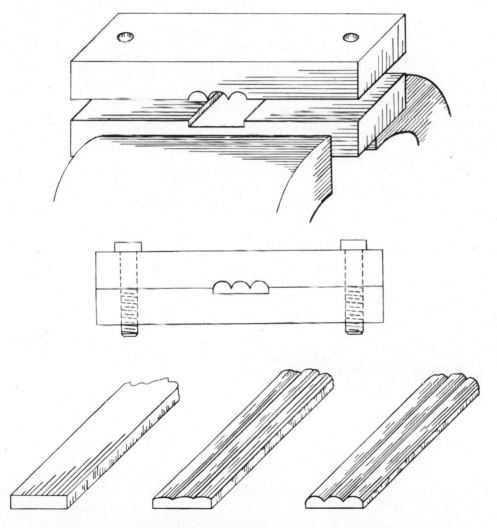

was ornamented by drawing it a number of times between two bars of steel, which were either bolted to the bench-top or pinched between the jaws of the vise. The bars were bolted together with a space between

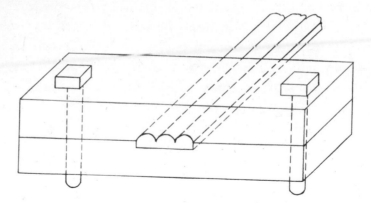

them of the size of the full band of silver. One bar was flat and the planned design was filled into the edge of the other. After each pass of the silver between the bars, they were drawn closer together until the full design was scraped into one side of the band.

Many cups had handles made of strips of silver, cut from reasonably thick slabs of metal. In cross-section they would have been square or rectangular. These strips were formed over suitably shaped stakes and soldered in place when the bottom band was applied to the cup.

Because considerable soldering was involved in the making of such articles as cups, mugs, and tankards, some consideration might be given to the procedure of soldering the various parts together. It is a general rule that solder should be easier to fuse than the metal intended to be soldered.

Simple and charming cup made by Benjamin Hiller of Boston late in the seventeenth century. The ornamented band on the bottom is not identical to the design in the directions, but was probably made by the same method. Height, $2\frac{13}{16}$ in.; diameter of top, $3\frac{1}{16}$ in.; diameter at base, $2\frac{5}{8}$ in. *Courtesy Henry Francis du Pont Winterthur Museum.*

This statement simply means that solder must have a lower melting point than the metals to be soldered. Solders preferably should have the same color as that of the metals to be joined, but this condition is rarely possible.

The most common solders are divided into two classes, hard and soft. The hard solders (used to solder silver), are ductile, will bear hammering without breaking, and are prepared partially of the metal which is to be soldered, with the addition of other metal by which a greater degree of fusibility is obtained. The hard solder for silver was composed of silver, copper, and zinc. It was sold to silversmiths in a granulated form, by the name of "spelter solder." Some silversmiths are thought to have made their own solder.

For successful soldering procedures the surface of the metals to be joined had to be clean and perfectly fitted together. The various parts were held together by soft iron binding wire. The cleaned surfaces were kept clean by applying a mixture of borax and water, borax being one of the items found in the inventories of silversmiths.

After all the preparations had been made, the object was held over a small, but very hot, forge fire until the solder flowed into the desired areas. Only minute amounts of solder were used, so that excesses did not have to be removed from conspicuous places; however, on obscure joints excessive quantities were often used and are still found.

If a beaker were really a large cup, it is very evident that the major difference in the production of the two objects was that a larger disk was needed to make the beaker. It might also be noted that, although some

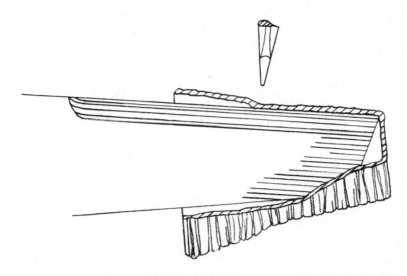

cups flared noticeably outward at the top, this characteristic is almost universal in regard to beakers. The flaring shape made them attractive because of their increased height and increased the rigidity of the top edge.

A great number of beakers were made in a variety of styles over a long span of years. Over five hundred, identified as products of American

Pair of beakers of the early eighteenth century with reeded bands applied at their bases. Made by Moody Russel (1694-1761), working at Barnstable, Massachusetts. Courtesy Metropolitan Museum of Art, The Sylmaris Collection, Gift of George Coe Graves, 1928.

craftsmen, are found in New England churches. The largest group of Colonial beakers has a plain cylindrical body with a flaring lip, and a molded band applied to the base. Such a style was popular in the sixteenth and seventeenth centuries in Holland and England, and probably accounts for the wide use in America in the eighteenth century.

Possibly the next form to evolve in America was the inverted bell shape, which flared at the top but receded to a smaller diameter at the bottom, to which a variety of bases were attached. One made by John Coney, inscribed with the date 1715, is owned by the Old South Church, Boston. A similarly shaped one with two handles is owned by the Church of Christ at Norwich, Connecticut. An example of the inverted bell shape by John Dixwell (1680-1725) of Boston, is fluted about one third of its height from the bottom and is mounted on an attractive molded band, which serves as a base. Jeremiah Dummer made a similar one; however, his is a bit more decorative, for he chose to spiral his fluting.

Throughout the century a continuous array of forms and ornamentation was presented by the craftsmen of the country. The tall Dutch style,

Pair of beakers made by Myer Myers. The strips of silver on the bottom edge of the beakers was drawn in a manner similar to the process used in making the like part for the cup. Myers made many other attractive objects of silver, but photographs of them are not available. *Courtesy Henry Francis du Pont Winterthur Museum*

An example of an attractive beaker made
by Samuel Kirk about 1825. The Samuel
Kirk Company is the oldest manufacturer
of silver objects in America. *Courtesy Henry
Francis du Pont Winterthur Museum.*

often called trumpet shaped, remained popular; some of these were pro-
fusely engraved. Myer Myers (1723-1795) of New York made a pair
late in the century in a classical form with straight sides similar to the
form of contemporary teapots. The straight-sided form was produced
in the nineteenth century, one bearing the mark of Samuel Kirk (1793-
1872), of Baltimore. The flaring sides of his product are straight and
both the top and bottom are ornamented by applied moldings in the
style of the late eighteenth century.

The interrelationship between form and function in an object is often
evident, as it is in a caudle cup. This vessel was really a hybrid form between a cup and a bowl, and although it was used for drinking, the contents might have been logically served from a bowl.

Most definitions of "caudle" explain it as a gruel, mixed with ale,
sweetened and spiced. Although this combination of ingredients sounds
rather palatable to the taste of the mid-twentieth-century man, it seems
less attractive when he learns that gruel is defined as "a drink made of
grain broths, often consisting of oatmeal, or malt drinks not hopped." It
is reported to have relaxed the drinker and was popular at occasions such
as weddings, feasts, baptisms, and funerals.

An extremely simple but charming caudle cup made by John Dixwell about 1698. The handles were cast or cut from strips of heavy silver and soldered to the body. The facets left by the planishing hammer can be faintly seen. Dixwell's mark is tastefully stamped near the top of the left handle. *Courtesy Henry Francis du Pont Winterthur Museum.*

Caudle cups are low vessels possibly three to four inches deep with about the same diameter. Their contour resembles the shape of a gourd with a bulbous body and the top third portion cut away to provide an opening for the vessel. The ones with lids closely resemble the shape of a complete gourd.

The method of constructing a caudle cup was very similar to the techniques used in making cups and beakers, except that the raising was done on a stake with a rounded, rather than a sharp, end. The sides were raised and planished, and some examples are known which have no ornamentation; however, if a repoussé design such as fluting was desired, the metal had to be annealed and the contour expanded from the inside by using a tool called a "snarling iron."

This procedure was done by using a "nurling iron," so-called in the inventory of Richard Conyers, but now termed a "snarling iron." This tool was made of a tapered piece of steel about eighteen inches long, square at the large end (possibly ¾ in. x ¾ in.) and tapering to a diameter of about one-fourth inch at the small end. The round small end was given a slight radius and bent, projecting upward about three inches.

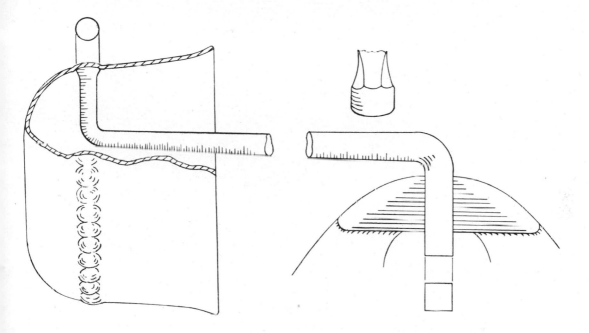

The square end was placed in a vise and the hollow vessel slipped over the opposite end, with only a very light pressure bearing it on the rounded end. By striking the bar in the top near the vise with a hammer, vibrations were created which simulated the effect of hammering the inner surface outward with a hammer but, of course, this area was so small it could not be reached with such a tool. A bulge of any desired shape and depth above the surface of the metal could be created by this procedure. The snarling iron was also used to increase the total diameter of such larger objects as teapots, when it could be more conveniently used than a hammer for such a purpose. The raised or repoussé area created by using the snarling iron was imprecise and, after sufficient height was obtained, the vessel was filled with pitch to give the surface of the metal some support, but also to permit a certain amount of resiliency. The repoussé design was then precisely defined on the outside of the vessel by using hammers, punches, and gravers; however, the total depth (similar

Caudle cup made by Jeremiah Dummer (1645-1718), Boston, Massachusetts. The cast handles were used also by two contemporaries of Dummer. The gadrooned pattern around the base was also popular at the time. *Courtesy Henry Francis du Pont Winterthur Museum.*

to bas-relief) was created from the inside. On some objects repoussé was sparingly used, while on others the entire surface seems to have been "worked." Repoussé work is usually associated with highly ornamented pieces, such as a Monteith bowl by John Coney, which John Marshall Phillips describes as "the most ambitious surviving piece by an American silversmith." *See page 97.*

Porringers and Bowls

Insofar as the function of an object, such as a teapot or a strainer, is evident from its shape and size, it is interesting to note that the identification of the role of one object of silver, namely, the porringer, has defied the ingenuity and imagination of historians for a long time.

The name, shape, and size of the vessel immediately suggests that it was used for serving porridge, or any other soft food appropriate for a child or an invalid. The use the child made of the porringer is still a matter of conjecture. The handle suggests he used it for drinking, but this hypothesis adds only another facet to be resolved in the mystery surrounding the object. The giving of porringers as gifts for children in modern times has perpetuated the idea that they are for the child's use. There does not seem to be any documented historical evidence for such a fact; at least, none has been found in this research into objects made of silver in the eighteenth century.

The flat bottom of the vessel suggests that it could be heated, possibly by a spirit lamp, but food was rarely cooked in silver vessels and drinks were heated by thrusting into them a hot poker of iron. It has been suggested that they might have been used for sugar before the advent of the covered sugar bowl, as were caudle cups and other low bowls.

The most bizarre theory is that surgeons carried a porringer in one pocket, and a lancet in another, both of which were used in the bleeding of patients. The lancet was used to puncture the blood vessel of the patient, and the porringer, pressed tightly against the body beneath the incision, caught the escaping blood. Bleeding was a common practice in Europe and America and, if a porringer were not used, some other vessel in general use was needed.

Regardless of their role, they are attractive objects, and few collectors

Silver porringer made by Jacobus van der Spiegel (1668-1708), of New York. This porringer has what might almost be called a standard bowl, for the shape of that portion changed very little throughout the time porringers were made. The delicate fret-work terminating in a heart-form is an attractive feature. *Courtesy Philadelphia Museum of Arts; photograph by A. J. Wyatt, staff photographer.*

of silver would regard their acquisitions complete without a few examples. As a matter of fact, they are so attractive that some collectors make a specialty of collecting them. They range in size from about four to six-and-a-half inches in diameter, with a corresponding variation in their depths. One of the largest extant is attributed to the great silversmith, John Coney, and many small ones can be seen in museums throughout the country. Very few have covers, although it is possible that many covers have been lost by owners who were indifferent to the value and importance of the treasures they possessed. Despite their size, shape, or function, they must have been useful vessels; one family inventory of the seventeenth century reported nine among their possessions.

The general shape of a porringer was that of a shallow open bowl with a flat base, slightly domed in the center. The sides closely approximated a half-circle with a narrow band flaring outward at the top. This band was an attractive feature; it could have served as a pouring lip, but its major purpose was probably to make the rim rigid for otherwise the edge would have been easy to bend. Although the shape of the porringer was pleasing, its greatest charm lay in the variety of handle forms. They will be discussed after the making of the bowl is detailed.

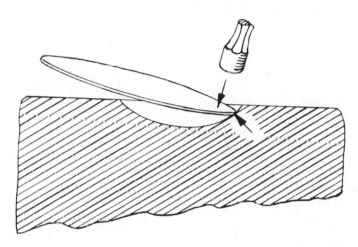

The porringer was made by the raising and/or stretching procedure, and thus the first step was to cut a disk of metal to the desired size. The band from the edge of the bottom to the edge of the disk was placed on the end grain of the tree trunk and slightly deepened by striking it with a hollowing hammer. When this process was finished, the object looked like a modern saucer.

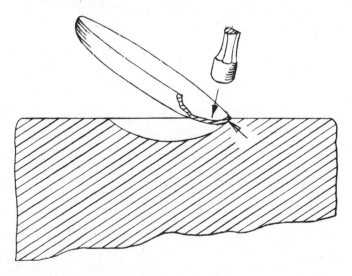

The problem of further deepening the bowl and reducing the diameter of the top was pursued as in the raising of a caudle cup, which the porringer closely resembled. The partially domed disk was then placed upside down on a stake and the sides raised, while the diameter of the top was simultaneously reduced.

After the desired shape of the sides was obtained, the semicircular form was planished and made smooth.

Next, the narrow edge of the top of the rim was bent outward on the edge of a stake with a sharp corner, and the inner portion of the bottom was domed on the end grain of a block of wood or a piece of lead. All of this work slightly distorted the levelness of the remaining part of the bottom, and this was made flat by applying pressure from the top.

The handles of porringers, most of them having only one, are by all odds their most exciting feature. They vary in size according to the size of the porringer, and are usually made of one piece of silver, possibly one-sixteenth to one-eighth inch in thickness. They are soldered to the bowl near the top edge. Some are horizontal while others bend upwards slightly; however, the position of those which angle upward might be the result of long use.

Bottom view of a silver porringer showing the common shape of the bowl and the way the handle was "butted" against the bowl for soldering. The design of this handle could have been formed by the casting process; however, the very small openings in other handles were probably punched or sawed. *Courtesy Henry Francis du Pont Winterthur Museum.*

There is a great variety in the designs, the quality of which gives them their charm. In the center of the handle was usually left a solid panel, on which the initials of the owner were often engraved. Around the panel were placed designs of endless variety, consisting of circles, hearts, quatrefoils, half-hearts, half-moons, and the like, and a confusion of scrolls which defy description. In later porringers a feature known as a "keyhole" came into extensive use by a number of silversmiths. This opening was placed at the end of the handle away from the bowl, and resembled the opening in an escutcheon used to decorate key holes in furniture.

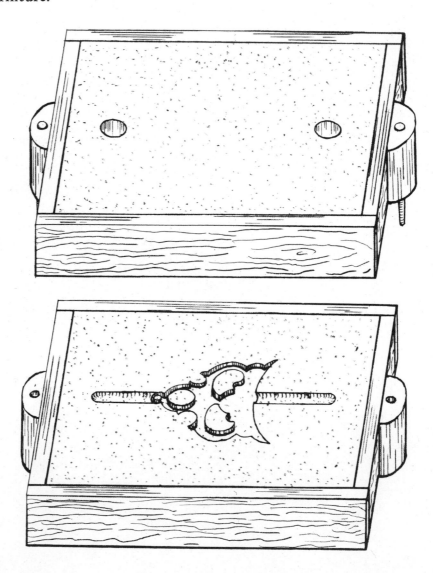

The designs in the handles were produced by a number of tools. The standard method for making holes, or openings, in sheet metal was with a punch, and this was doubtless a very popular one because, in addition to an opening, some form could be given to it by using a punch with an appropriate shape. It is evident that much filing and engraving was done after the openings were made, for punching was not a precision process and there was probably no more noticeable evidence of a slovenly silversmith than a poorly wrought handle on a porringer. It is also known that some were cast with the openings in them.

In casting a handle for a silver porringer a "pattern" of wood was first made which was a replica of the intended handle. This pattern was then placed in the middle between two boxes, called a "flask," which had neither tops nor bottoms. Sand was rammed tightly into them, enclosing the pattern, so the parts of the flask could be handled without the sand falling out.

Vertical openings were cut through the sand to the center of the flask, the two halves were separated, the pattern removed, and the flask reassembled. The thinness of the handle required that the sand be dried so the molten metal would not be unduly chilled as it flowed through its intended course. Molten metal was then poured into one of the vertical openings. It dropped to the center of the flask, filled the cavity created by the pattern, and rose in the second vertical opening.

After the handle cooled it was removed from the sand, the excess metal was removed, and the handle finished by filing and polishing.

The widest part of the handle was usually set against the bowl for aesthetic and practical reasons. A long stretch of metal joining the bowl

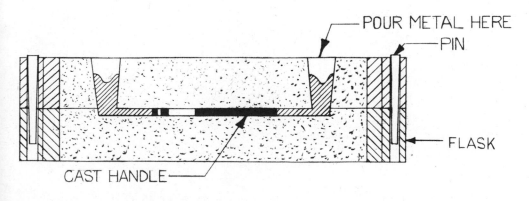

SECTION

made the juncture strong and rigid, which was important then, for planned obsolesence was not a common practice in those times. After the proper fit was achieved, the usual flux and hard solder was applied, followed by heating until the solder flowed throughout the joint. Finally, unwanted tool marks, such as those left by a file, were removed, the object was properly polished, and it was ready for a wealthy patron to step inside the door of the silversmith's shop.

Porringers with "key-hole" handles reached the zenith of their popularity about the middle of the eighteenth century; however, they continued to be made to the end of the century. The earlier examples had openings in the now solid center portion of the handle. These openings were a vestige of an earlier style made in America and England. This example was made by Richard Humphreys (c. 1722-1791) of Philadelphia. *Courtesy Philadelphia Museum of Art.*

Although the word "bowl" is in common usage today, a search into the references of the eighteenth century reveals that the word was not as generally applied to vessels then as it is now. The only definition found in a publication of the eighteenth century is in the *Encyclopedia: or, a Dictionary of Arts, Science and Miscellaneous Literature,* published by Thomas Dobson, Philadelphia, 1798. Curiously the definition there refers to the word first in its relation to a game by saying that, "BOWL, denotes either a ball of wood, for the use of bowling; or a vessel of capacity, wherein to hold liquors."

The definition in the *Oxford English Dictionary,* 1933, not only continues the confusion of the use of the sphere or spherically shaped object, but also the spelling of the word. It points out that as early as A.D. 1000 a Saxon word "bollan" was used to describe a vessel for holding water, and specifically points out that:

> The normal modern spelling would be BOLL which came down to the 17 c. in the sense of 'round vessel', and is still used in the sense of 'round seed-vessel'; but the early ME. pronounciation of -oll as owl (cf., roll, poll, toll, etc.) has left its effects in the modern sense of 'vessel' which is thus at once separated in form from other senses of its own (see BOLL sb[1]), and confounded with BOWL sb[2] a ball, from the Fr. boulee.
>
> A (round) vessel to hold liquids, rather wide than deep; distinguished from a cup, which is rather deep than wide. Usually hemispherical or nearly so.

It is, of course, evident that a porringer is a bowl and thus might not have been given any singular consideration; however, its unique shape and mysterious uses suggested that such matters be emphasized. Other uses for bowls were for holding punch, sugar, sauces, posset, or for serving berries.

A discussion regarding the making of a low bowl might logically start with the techniques used to produce a vessel called a "shallow drinking bowl" in the collection of silver objects at the Henry Francis du Pont Winterthur Museum.

Because this bowl is round, the silversmith chose a disk of silver and started pounding it over the well-beaten trunk of a tree, heretofore frequently mentioned. Because the sides do not turn inward, and the object

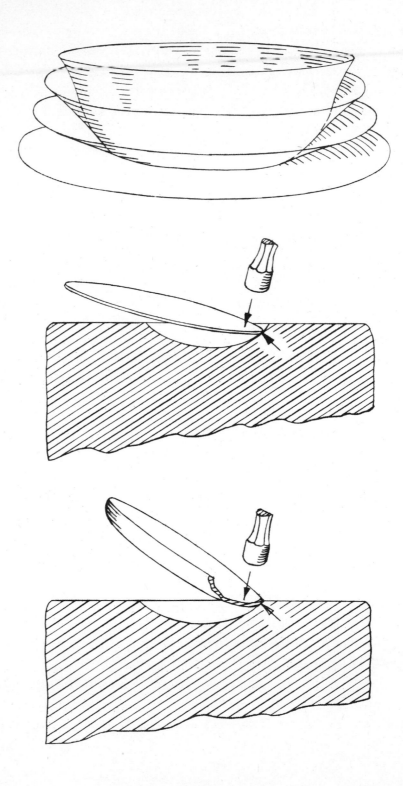

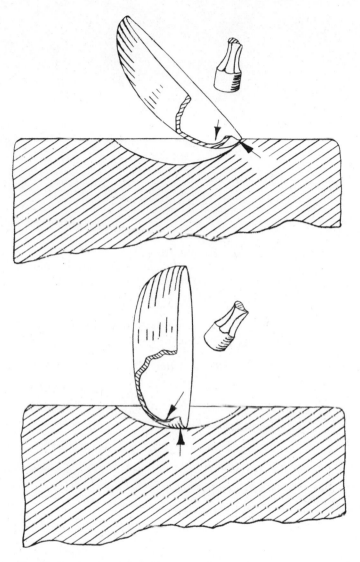

is not very deep, it is possible that much of the shaping could be done with a hollowing hammer on the tree trunk. The disk was struck with a hammer in concentric circles, starting at the outside and working inward to the edge of the bottom, which remained flat. After each complete "pass" of hammer blows from the outer edge inward, the disk was slightly changed so that the form was actually depressed through tensional stretching until the desired depth was obtained. This work distorted the surface of the metal; to restore it a planishing hammer was used.

Shallow drinking bowl believed to have been made by Henricus Boelen about 1690, in New York. The modest style of the decoration seems very well suited to the vessel to which it was applied. Height, $1\frac{9}{16}$ in.; diameter at top, $4\frac{5}{8}$ in. *Courtesy Henry Francis du Pont Winterthur Museum.*

The decoration of this particular bowl was done by a technique called chasing. The bowl was filled with pitch, and the desired design drawn on the outer surface of the metal. Then, with a chasing hammer and a wide variety of special chisels and punches, the design was slowly pounded below the surface of the bowl, but no metal was removed in this decorative process, and no areas were raised from the inside as was done in repoussé. One of the most common uses of this technique was in the decorating of lids for warming pans made of copper or brass. The design is almost as equally evident on the bottom as on the top of the lid; however, the detail is not as precise on the bottom. Generally speaking, this technique required less skill than other modes of decorating, such as engraving or repoussé.

The production of this bowl by John Coney probably required all the knowledge and techniques at the command of this very skilled silversmith. John Marshall Phillips, one of the outstanding connoisseurs of American silver in modern times, described this bowl as "the most ambitious surviving piece by an American silversmith." Coney was a master-craftsman and it is not surprising that he should have produced such a *chef-d'oeuvre. Courtesy Yale University Art Gallery, Mabel Brady Garvan Collection*

It is likely that most silversmiths chased their own products, but the following advertisement from the *Pennsylvania* (Philadelphia) *Packet*, July 13, 1772, indicates that at least one man was a professional chaser.

JOHN ANTHONY BEAU

A celebrated Chaser, in Fourth street, opposite the new Lutheran Church, being lately arrived in this city from Geneva, Takes this method to recommend himself to the favour of all the Public, and acquaints them that he performs all sorts of chasing work in gold, silver, and other metals, such as watch cases, coffee and tea pots, sugar boxes, cream pots, tea., in the gentlest and newest taste. All persons who will honour him with their employment in any such work, may be assured that he will use his utmost endeavours to give them universal satisfaction. He likewise offers his services to teach ladies drawing, and to give them the best principles to learn very soon, let it be figures, ornaments, flowers, or designs for embroidering, etc., all at reasonable prices, and such hours as best suits the scholars.

Most low bowls have two handles mounted opposite each other. Some were made of several strands of wire twisted together, others were made of strips or squares of silver, and some craftsmen twisted the squares to give an effect of roundness, which was decorative and comfortable to hold. A few examples have handles that were cast. They were shaped in a variety of forms and attached by using the customary "silver solder."

There were, of course, an endless variety of bowls made of silver, for many uses. Many of them are usually referred to as punch bowls, particularly the larger ones which might have been logically used for such a purpose. Some were simply hemispherical in shape with a molded top edge and a heavy molded foot such as one made by Myer Myers. Others, such as the famous Sons of Liberty bowl by Paul Revere, Jr., have a very subtle reverse curve in their side contour without a molded edge at the top, but a very substantial molded base. The zenith of American silversmithing in the eyes of John Marshall Phillips was reached in a Monteith bowl by John Coney.

These bowls were designed with concave scallops around the top edge presumably named for a fanatical Scot, Monsieur Monteith, who wore a cloak with similar notches in the bottom edge. The notches reputedly served to hold the bases of wine glasses which dipped inward into cold

Silver "slop bowl" of the Federal period made by Samuel Williamson who worked in Philadelphia from 1794 until 1813. The mirror-like finish indicates that he was an expert planisher, and the beaded edges are a Philadelphia "bench-mark." *Courtesy Philadelphia Museum of Art; photograph by A. J. Wyatt, staff photographer*

water or ice, preliminary to using them for drinking. The highly ornamented top edge was often constructed so that it could be removed and thus a plain-topped bowl for other purposes became available.

Mugs and Tankards

Of all the terms applied to vessels used for drinking, the word "tankard" is probably more loosely used than any other. This situation arises from the fact that a tankard is a vessel with prestige; the common and unwarranted use of the word in the market place suggests that the merchant is attempting to assign qualities to vessels which in reality they do not possess. The license for such indiscriminate use arises from the fact that references of the eighteenth century rarely define the words "mug" and "tankard," and those which do are imprecise about significant and distinguishing details. The distinction is clearly pointed out in *Zell's Popular Encyclopedia*, Philadelphia, 1871, which states that a tankard is "a large vessel for the reception of liquors; also a drinking mug with a cover, as a tankard of London porter." The clue to the difference is that the tankard has a *cover*. This definition does not imply that no other similar vessels have covers, for flagons do, but they are not regarded as being vessels for drinking and they usually have a larger capacity than that of a tankard.

The difference between a mug and a tankard seems unimportant to the uninitiated, for they both were used for drinking, and, it is important to note, similar techniques were used to make the bodies of the two.

To make a mug with straight flaring sides, the silversmith started with a disk of annealed silver and hollowed the form over a tree trunk, as previously explained. He then turned the disk upside down and began raising the sides, simultaneously reducing the diameter of the disk toward the top. Thus far the analogy parallels the making of a cup or beaker.

One would expect that the craftsman continued to reduce the diameter of the mug toward the top until the final desired diameter of the mug was achieved. If this procedure were followed, the mug, like the cup,

would have been made of one solid piece of metal. However, in none of the mugs examined by the writer was such a procedure followed.

The sides were raised until the diameter of the top of the workpiece was the intended diameter of the base of the mug. The shape flared outward toward the top. At this point the bottom of the piece was removed and, because it retained its original thickness, it was thick enough to be stretched and provide a bottom for the large end. In the meantime, the

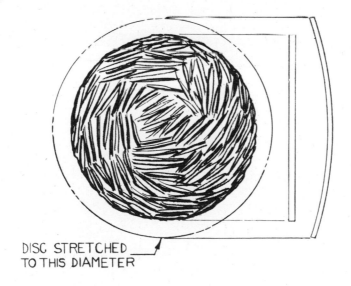

DISC STRETCHED
TO THIS DIAMETER

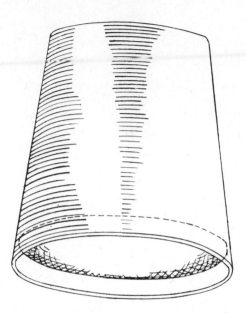

shell was inverted so that the small end was at the top and the large diameter at the bottom. After the disk was stretched, it was bowed inward and soldered into the bottom of the mug. The bottom was raised a bit from the very bottom of the shell so that it did not touch the table top when it rested in its natural position.

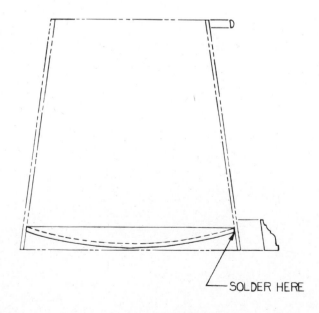

SOLDER HERE

The top edge of the mug could be made thicker and more rigid by caulking, or it could be reinforced by applying a molding, produced in a manner similar to the one used to create the band for the bottom of the cup or by a swage. A heavier molding was made and applied to the bottom edge of the mug. Both moldings were attached by the use of hard solder, which provided virtually a permanent joint between all parts.

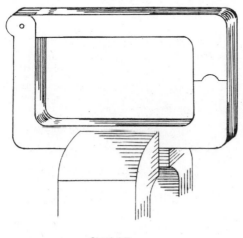

SWAGE

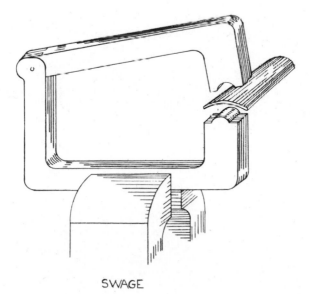

SWAGE

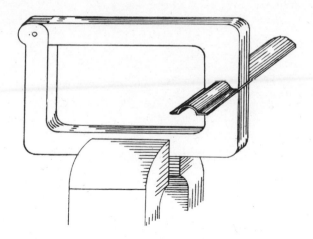

The handles of mugs throughout the seventeenth and early eighteenth centuries were strips (or straps) of silver, similar to those used on cups, except that they were wider and thicker because a mug was a bigger vessel. They were cut from heavy pieces of silver and shaped for a comfortable grip.

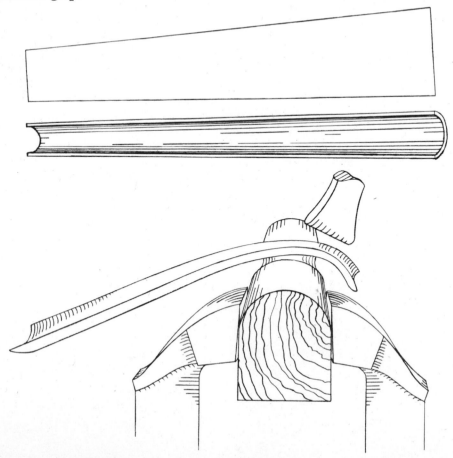

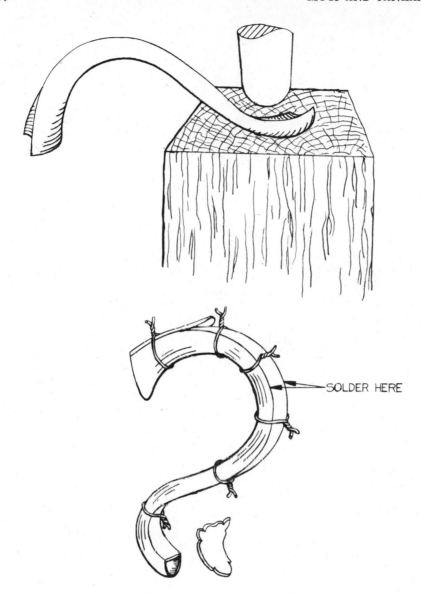

SOLDER HERE

As the amenities of life improved in the eighteenth century, changes were reflected in the objects made, particularly those of silver, for their status reflected that of the affluent society. The flat band continued to be used, but underneath it a half-round band was attached to increase the cross-sectional size of the handle and make it more comfortable to hold. This procedure more than doubled the quantity of silver needed, and greatly increased the cost, for the fabrication of such a handle re-

quired much time. The top end of the handle lay flush against the side
of the mug, but the bottom flared away and terminated in a fancy form
created by the addition of a small plate, attractively shaped. Later, a band
encircled the mug, dividing the side into two sections, the bottom a bit
shorter than the top. Cyphers and other decorative motifs were engraved
on the sides.

The image of silver tankards is unique among objects made of this
metal, for, as a group, they are probably the most desirable to own. It
must be pointed out, however, that several other single pieces surpass
any tankard in prestige. Among these objects, well known today, is the
bowl made by Paul Revere for his fifteen fellow members of the Sons
of Liberty. This bowl was made on the eve of the Revolution and is inscribed (engraved) with appropriate sentiments, as well as the names of
the members. Another object rich in its historical association is the inkstand made by Philip Syng, Jr., in 1752 for the assembly of Pennsylvania.
Its significance arises from the fact that it was used by the signers of
the Declaration of Independence and of the Constitution. Although it
is not an extravagant masterpiece of workmanship, it is difficult for the
imagination to conceive a more important use for an object of any metal
by any American craftsman.

A fitting introduction to the tankard of the late seventeenth and early eighteenth century might be an excerpt from *American Silver* by John Marshall Phillips:

> The most popular drinking vessel, judging from inventories in an age "potent in potting," was the cider or ale tankard, with its straight tapering body reenforced by a moulded base and rim, a low flat cover, raised by a horizontal ram's horn, or cupped thumbpiece, and a massive scroll handle terminating in a shield. . . .
>
> The usual capacity was a quart but two larger examples are known, one by Jeremiah Dummer, the other by his master, Robert Sanderson, fashioned for Isaac and Mary Vergoose. [One is known to have been made by Benjamin Hiller of full gallon capacity.]

Close attention to details of shape and construction reveals that the body portions of tankards and mugs with straight sides were very similar in the early eighteenth century. Both were similarly raised from a disk of metal with the sides flaring outward, after which the bottom was removed. Because it retained its original thickness, the bottom could be stretched until it was large enough to cover the wide end of the flaring cylinder, it having been inverted in both cases. Both had reinforcing bands applied at the top and bottom edges, but the tankard was supplied with a lid and a thumbpiece, while the mug was not.

Throughout most of the first half of the century, the lids of tankards were low with flat tops. They were formed by using a disk of silver with the same diameter as that of the intended final dimension of the lid. The

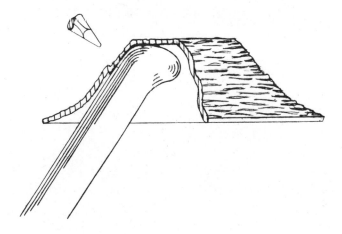

inner portion of the lid was deepened over the edge of a piece of hard wood with a sinking or hollowing hammer, in a manner similar to that employed in the making of a plate. A reasonably wide, flat edge was retained, as in the plate, and the bulge, or booge, was planished to make it smooth and uniform in roundness. Usually, a small offset was created at the bottom of the bulge, which gave the lid a finished appearance. The embryonic lid was then turned upside down when placed on the tankard, with a portion of the flat edge overhanging the sides of the vessel. A crenelated design was sometimes cut into the edge of the lid at the front, to further enhance its elegance.

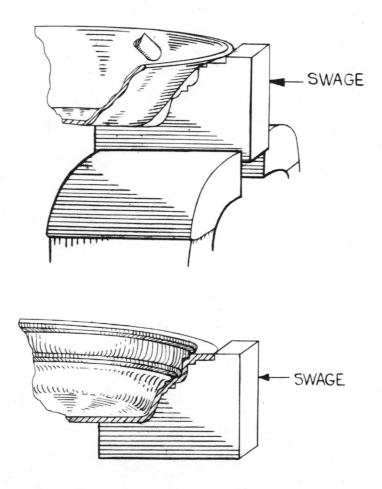

Swage used in making a dome-shaped lid for a tulip-shaped tankard. *See page 112.*

After the lid was formed, it was placed over the opening in the top of the vessel, and preparations were made for attaching the two together. A thumbpiece was made by casting a design in sand or cuttlebone, and a hinge strap was formed by casting or hammering a piece of heavy silver into the desired shape. It should be noted that although both these parts served an important function as parts of the tankard, they were equally important for the decorative touch they added to the vessel. Knuckles forming a hinge were fashioned in one end of each of these parts, with a pin running through them, so that the various parts could be disengaged, if necessary. The joints in the hinge had to be meticulously filed and fitted, so that smooth and unrestricted action between the lid and the body was possible. (There should be no reason to create frustrated drinkers.) If a presumably old piece does not show normal wear on the hinge knuckles, certain doubts could arise concerning its authenticity or its age. (It seems rather evident that our ancestors were frequent drinkers.) A long, tapering body drop was often attached to the bottom of the handle, to enrich the design and make attachment to the body more secure.

Possibly one of the final operations in the making of the handle assembly was to file the bottom end of the handle to accept the desired fitting. The designs of these finials varied with each maker; however, such shapes as shields and cherubs' heads were popular with many craftsmen. Obviously, some finials were very simply made, while others were masterpieces of the craftsman's art. The last act before soldering was to cut or file a hole in the very bottom of the scroll end of the handle, to allow the heated and expanding air to escape; otherwise, it was virtually impossible to make a perfect soldered joint between the handle and the body of the tankard.

Soldering the handle and the thumbpiece to the tankard was done in separate operations. The thumbpiece was attached to the lid, and the handle was secured to the body at two points. If every procedure went according to plan, a pin was then forced through the knuckles of the hinge, and the tankard was ready for final polishing and the market place.

The description of this straight-sided, flat-topped, low tankard should not lead the reader to conclude that only such types were made in the eighteenth century. Although the techniques of the silversmith permitted a very quick response to changes in style, unlike the pewterer who had invested in expensive molds which he was loathe to discard, it is very evident that traditional styles in silver lingered on, usually with several transitional changes, until a clearly new design evolved. For example, in 1768 Paul Revere continued to make straight-sided tankards, although they were taller and thinner than those of the early style, and had a domed lid usually associated with a later style in tankards. A flame-like finial was mounted on top of the lid and a molding encircled the body, a feature rarely found on the early tankard.

Nor must one suppose that all those of the early type were plain and unornamented. In the collection of the Henry Francis du Pont Winterthur Museum is a tankard with a hinge strap in the design of a lion's head; a cherub's head graces the bottom end of the handle, and a cut-leaf border surrounds its base. This example was made by Jacob Boelen (1657-1729) of New York for Everett and Engeletie Wendell of Albany, who were married in 1710. Their initials are engraved in block letters on the handle in the traditional pattern of a triangle, with the W at the

Straight-sided tankard made by Jacob Boelen of New York, probably early in the eighteenth century. The cocoon-shaped thumbpiece, the cast decorations, and the cut-leaf border design are typical features of early tankards made in New York. Height, 7⅛ in; diameter at base, 5⅜ in.; diameter at top, 4¾ in. *Courtesy Henry Francis du Pont Winterthur Museum.*

Tankards showing a variety in body shape and size, as well as in the appendages, such as handles, lids, thumbpieces, bases, and handle endings. The largest tankard was made by Benjamin Hiller of Boston late in the seventeenth century, and is a full gallon capacity; height, 10⅜ in. The smallest example was made by Elias Pelletreau (1726-1810) of New York. The pear-shaped (tulip-shaped) one was made by Phillip Syng, Jr., of Philadelphia, (1703-1789).

Courtesy Henry Francis du Pont Winterthur Museum

Tulip-shaped tankard made by Philip Syng, Jr., of Philadelphia about 1750. Although this piece might be described as elegant, there is evidence of the Quaker taste for simplicity to be found in it. *Courtesy Philadelphia Museum of Art*

top, under which are placed the two E's. In addition to engraving, the techniques of chasing and repoussé were sparingly used to decorate tankards throughout the eighteenth century in America.

Possibly the most extravagant form of ornamentation used on tankards in the early part of the century was a technique previously called "cut-leaf," but usually referred to as "cut-card." The presence of such work

The Gift of Mary Bartlett Widow of Eph.ᵐ Bartlett to the third Church in Brookfeild. 1768

Tankards made by Paul Revere for the Brookfield Church. The inscription confirms the donor and the date. This is the only entry for six tankards recorded in the existing account books of Paul Revere. *Courtesy Henry Francis du Pont Winterthur Museum*

on tankards made in New York can be easily explained by the fact that it was a very popular form of decoration in Holland in earlier times. It could have come to America directly from Holland, or possibly via England, where it was also favored among silversmiths in the second half of the seventeenth century.

The term "cut-card" arises from the fact that the decoration appears to be a series of cutouts, like small cards, which were usually applied above the band encircling the bottoms of tankards and beakers. Later, the designs were cut into the edge of a strip of metal, instead of on separate pieces.

The strip was easier to manage in the soldering operation, particularly because interstices had to be clean and uncluttered with excess solder. If surplus solder did manage to fill joints inadvertently, of course, the deft hand of the silversmith could remove it with a graver.

Additions, such as veins and linear designs, could be added to the outside contour to enrich the effect, and, if the whole work were cleverly done, it sometimes appeared as if another technique were used, such as repoussé. The tolerant attitude of the British toward the fine Dutch craftsmanship in New York permitted the craftsmen to continue their traditional techniques after the British took over the city in 1665.

Although the straight-sided, flat-topped tankard is highly prized by collectors today, the fastidious and affluent patrons of the mid-eighteenth century probably learned of a new style of tankard. This new style is discussed in *Historic Silver of the Colonies and Its Makers,* by Francis Bigelow, who describes it as it was about to invade America:

> In the middle of the eighteenth century the tankard with a "bellied" or bulbous body, a domed cover, and a high moulded foot, with and without a moulding encircling the body, came into vogue in England, and its popularity was the greatest in the third quarter of the century. Today this form is frequently described as pear or tulip-shaped.

Any observer who has given serious consideration to the evolution of styles in any media would know that the bulbous-bodied tankard did not appear "overnight." Nor was the transition in style confined to tankards, or to any field of the decorative arts. The early flat-topped tankard was compatible with the furnishings of medieval times, which lingered long with the aristocracy of England, and subsequently were popular in America when the country was first settled. Although the image of the colonist is usually one of poverty, inventories of estates of the seventeenth century reveal substantial accumulations of silverplate. Naturally, the first tankards made here were replicas of those the silversmiths saw about them, sides flared outward, in the style to which the patron was accustomed. Unlike today, the potential buyer of a tankard probably did not urge the silversmith to create a form which was new and different from the status quo. The evolution was slow, but the flat top was eventually discarded for a domed one, bands of molding encircled the bodies, and decorative motifs were more widely used. Finally, a style was evolved that was light in appearance, graceful in line, and completely compatible with the walnut and mahogany furnishings in the style of Queen Anne and the Georges.

Despite the grace and beauty of the tankard with a bulbous-shaped body, not many were made in America. This curious situation could not be attributed to the inadequacy of the silversmith, for most of them were very highly skilled men. Few new tools or processes were involved in their making, and the prestige of the latest English styles seems to have been evident at that time in all the furnishings of the house.

Craftsmen had been making straight-sided tankards with domed lids, there was no drastic change in the style of the handle, and the body was not greatly different from those being made for caudle cups. The technique for making the base was essentially the same as the one used for the lid; however, some adaptation had to be made to fit the part to the flat bottom of the body.

Shaping the body was started by placing the disk of metal over the well-beaten tree stump, where hammer blows were applied concentrically from the outer edge to the edge of the bottom, which remained flat. It has been pointed out that this type of tensional stretching had limitations, although considerable depth could be achieved before the craftsman had to move his work to the outside of the vessel. With a raising hammer and appropriate stakes, he simultaneously reduced the diameter of the disk and raised the side to the desired depth. This work is done by compressional stretching, which is a very versatile technique by which the shaping of the metal can be minutely controlled. Finally, the whole body had to be planished to remove the distortions created by the raising

process, and the top edge was caulked (made thicker than the body by beating it with a hammer). The increased thickness made the edge more rigid, and gave the craftsman an opportunity to create a design there which merged the body and the lid into one attractive design unit.

To make the base, the craftsman again laid the disk of metal on the tree trunk and created a dish-shaped object with a flat bottom. Then he inverted the piece and brought it as close as possible to the desired shape and size by raising it over a round stake with a radius on the end.

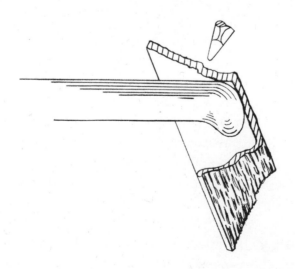

It is obvious that now the base was roughly shaped but lacked the
ogee design which is the major design element in such bases. To produce
this feature, the silversmith used a tool called a swage. This implement

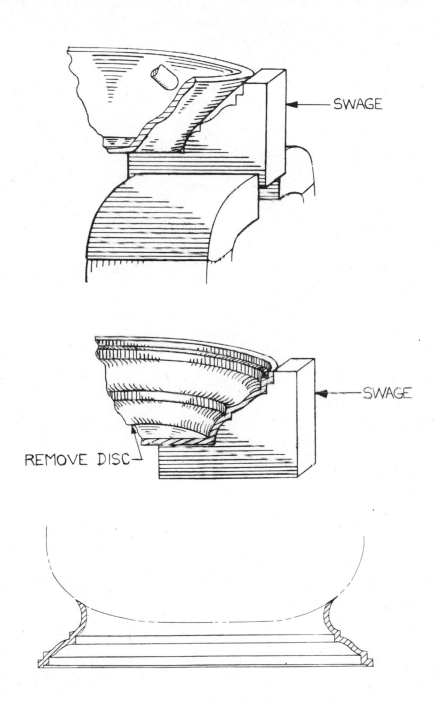

was made of iron or steel plate, possibly three eighths of an inch thick, into which the profile of the desired shape was filed. It was pinched tightly in a vise and, as the disk was rotated over its edge, the silver was slowly beaten with hammers and punches until the finished product was formed. Swages were very common tools in the eighteenth century, being used by craftsmen in other metal trades as well. Finally, the flat bottom was removed, the upper portion of the form turned outward, and fitted to the bottom of the tankard and soldered in place.

Teapots and Coffeepots

The evolution in the style and the size of the teapot was greatly influenced by the social customs prevailing in the various countries in which hot tea was consumed. Because the social conventions and technological processes in most areas of early America came almost exclusively from England, one must explore the early use of tea in that country. It is known that the English custom of tea-drinking began in the second quarter of the seventeenth century. At that time its price was exorbitant, being six to ten pounds for sixteen ounces, and it was used mostly for medicinal purposes. As it became cheaper, its magic influence on the health of the drinker probably diminished, in spite of which the great English custom of drinking tea became widespread. Samuel Pepys records in his diary of 1660 that he sent out for a cup of tea, "a China drink of which I had never drunk before."

It is easy to understand that in the beginning, because of its limited use, no special vessel existed for dispensing it, and those extant at that time were interchangeably used, as reported by Francis Bigelow in *Historic Silver of the Colonies and Its Makers*:

> At first apparently no difference in size was made in the English teapot, coffee pot, and chocolate pot; but after several years the teapot was made lower than the coffee pot and chocolate pot and in later years broader. In the late nineteenth century teapots were made in many different shapes.

The earliest form to become popular in America was influenced by a contemporary style in England, a pear-shaped vessel in the style of Queen Anne. At least one such pot, which was made by John Coney of Boston (1655-1722), has survived.

American silver teapot, early eighteenth century, by John Coney. Engraved with arms of Jean Paul Mascarine. Height, 7⅛ in. *Courtesy Metropolitan Museum of Art. Bequest of A. T. Clearwater, 1933.*

Although this pear-shaped style became a very sophisticated form later in the eighteenth century, the one made by Coney was obviously an embryonic type, well wrought but not particularly pleasing from an aesthetic point of view. There is a crude relationship between the different parts of the body, which had no ornamentation except for the coat-of-arms of one of the owners engraved on the side. The spout is small and tight against the body, the handle is large with only a thumbpiece protruding from its semicircular contour, the base is small and barely evident, and the knob on the lid does no more than conform to the

over-all simple pattern of the piece. The hinge is very small and close
to the lip of the pot, and was designed only for function without add-
ing to the intended design of the pot. The only part that seems to have
been specifically ornamented is the spout, which is in the form of a gooseneck. In spite of these deficiencies, this style of pot is compatible with
that of contemporary tankards and is very attractive in the eyes of
many connoisseurs.

The shape of the body is very similar to that of some caudle cups and
both were probably made in a similar manner. A disk of metal was placed
on the end of a tree stump and struck with a hollowing hammer until
a saucerlike contour was obtained. It was then inverted and placed on a

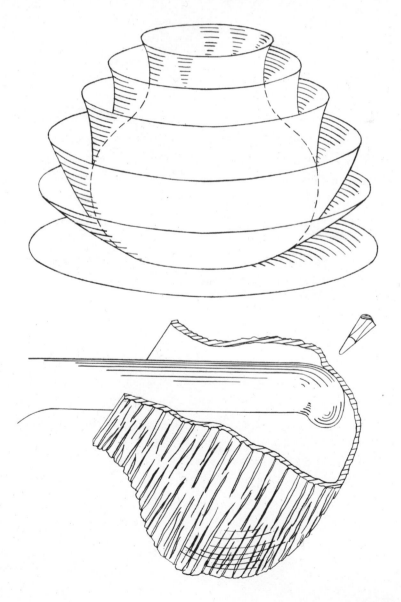

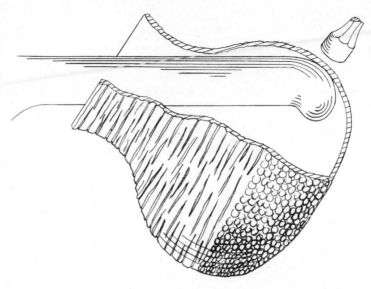

stake with a round end, the outer edge being contracted with a raising
(cross-peen) hammer until the desired depth was achieved, as well as
the desired diameter of the opening of the vessel. The edge was caulked
to increase its thickness and provide adequate metal for forming the lip
of the pot. The lid was made in a similar way; however, the knob was
shaped by "turning" it on a lathe. It is probable that a man as experienced
and well equipped as Coney owned a lathe; however, because it was a
facility little needed by a silversmith, most other craftsmen had their
turnings made by a professional "turner." One of these was Thomas
Gregory, who placed the following advertisement in the *Pennsylvania*
(Philadelphia) *Gazette,* on May 3, 1753.

THOMAS GREGORY

In Third-street, Philadelphia, opposite Church-alley and near
Market-street, Makes and sells all sorts of brass work suitable for
mills, heads for dogs, brass dogs, shovels and tongs, candlesticks of
all sorts, chaise and chair furniture, gun furniture of all sorts, spoon
moulds, shoe buckles, bell metal skillets and kettles, house and horse
bells, and a variety of other, things too tedious to mention, at the
most reasonable rates.

N.B. The said Gregory turns all sorts of iron, brass, pewter and silver; likewise gives the best price for old brass, and mends all sorts of
brass work.

The handle was made of wood because of its low conductivity of heat; then, too, its rich dark texture made a pleasing contrast with the bright luster of the silver. It was almost semicircular in shape, and was attached to the pot by tenons which were inserted into two flaring cylinders. Pins, crosswise in each cylinder, held the handle of wood firmly in place. The outer ends of the cylinders were banded to make them attractive, to make them rigid, and to create a pleasing transition from the metal to the wood.

The technique used in making the spout is somewhat shrouded in mystery; however, it could have been made by one of three methods. It could have been cast in halves, and this was entirely possible, for andirons and candlesticks of brass were made by this method throughout the

Globular teapot made by Jacob Hurd of Boston about 1750. Wood is used in the knob and for the handle because of its nonconductivity of heat. The spout is mounted very high on the pot, but as a whole this example is attractive. This style has a great deal of prestige, for a portrait of Paul Revere by John Copley shows the craftsman holding such a pot. *Courtesy Henry Francis du Pont Winterthur Museum*

eighteenth century. Or each half could have been pounded in a swage of iron, thus requiring two swages to make the two halves of the spout. Or it could have been made from a sheet of silver, cut to a prescribed flat pattern and shaped into a cylinder with bends at the top and bottom.

To make a swage a pattern of the spout first had to be made of wood, with provision to separate it into halves through the middle. By using each half separately, a cavity was formed in iron in the reverse of the exterior of the pattern. A piece of silver, larger than the cavity, was laid over it and beat down until the general outline of the form was achieved. Next, a heavy sheet of lead was laid over the silver and struck with a hammer until the silver was forced into the small contours without cracking the metal on the high ridges. This method gave an almost finished surface to the exterior of the spout; however, the outer interstices had to be made sharp and clean with files and gravers after the silver was removed from the swage. The edges of the joint between the halves were fitted perfectly, and the two halves were then soldered together. The solder used for this operation had a reasonably high melting point, so that the joint did not "open" when the spout was soldered to the pot.

A flat circular band of silver, possibly three eighths of an inch wide, was fitted to the bottom and soldered in place to keep the pot in an upright position. This very simple base was compatible with the design of the pot and enhanced its aesthetic quality. After all the parts were attached, the pot was polished with pumice to remove scratches and evidences of fabrication, and finally rottenstone was used to give the metal its maximum luster.

Although the teapot by Coney has unmistakable charm, it is very evident that its lack of ornamentation and stubby form were somewhat incompatible with the light and elegant house furnishings of the later portion of the eighteenth century. There is evidence in a similar pot made by I. Ten Eyck, of New York, that an inevitable progression in style was occurring. His domed cover had a molded band, while the body had an incised band at the point where the exterior form changed from convex to concave. The gooseneck spout extended farther from the body and terminated at the top in a form described as a "snake's head." The hinge connecting the lid with the body was placed a greater distance from the body than on the Coney pot, with the result that it now became a prominent decorative and functional part of the pot. Wood was used, not only for the handle, but also in the knob of the lid, where its quality

Teapot in the Queen Anne style made by Daniel Christian Fueter, New York, about 1760. The body was shaped from a disk, starting on the end grain of a tree stump and then raising it over a stake. It was brought to its final shape by careful planishing, the marks often being more evident on the inside surface than on the outside. The case and the lid were both started on a tree stump but the final detailed finish and form was achieved by hammering, using a swage. Height, 7¾ in. *Courtesy Henry Francis du Pont Winterthur Museum*

of not conducting heat must have been appreciated by all who used the vessel. Ten Eyck did retain the simple base used by Coney, but it, too, finally lost status, and a molded base similar to the one used on tankards with a bulbous-shaped body came into popular fashion.

It is interesting to note that globular-shaped teapots were also made in America. These really needed molded bases to enhance what was otherwise an unattractive form. Little imagination was required to envision the molded base of the globular teapot on the pear-shaped one, and a number of silversmiths produced such vessels with what might be called a "stunning" result.

The form of the pear-shaped teapot, like most of the other forms of the period, became quite refined and made by the same methods of other objects about the middle of the eighteenth century. There was a marked difference in the diameter of various parts of the body of the pot, the molding around the lid was made more pronounced, the cross-section shape of the spout was sometimes paneled instead of being elliptical or round, and the molded base was added. The spout continued to be mounted low, as it should have been but was not always on the globular form, and the entire pot could be described as an harmonious and attractive creation in silver. It might be pointed out that the form rarely was ornamented in the rococo style so widely used on other vessels in the third quarter of the eighteenth century.

There was virtually no change in the techniques used to produce such pots from the making of the tulip-shaped tankard. An old exercise was adapted for the making of the molded base, which is explained in the survey relating to the manufacturing ("making by hand") of tankards.

By mid-century some containers were being made for sugar and cream, but the tea set *per se* did not appear on a grand scale until the final quarter of the period, which was dominated by the making of objects from sheet silver, and is generally called the "Classical Period." This was the era when the Revere star neared its zenith, but to many critics the craft of silversmithing began to lose the luster it had achieved at mid-century.

At this point in the discussion of the materials, tools, techniques, and products of the silversmith, it must be recognized that there were constants and variables in the trade throughout the eighteenth century. For example, there was no change in the metal and very little in the tools, but there certainly were innovations in the style of the product and in methods of production. Before proceeding with some of the fundamental changes, most of which occurred in the second half of the century, it should be noted that, as a whole, the eighteenth century might be regarded as the "Golden Era" of silversmithing in America. In most cases the workmanship was superior, the objects were exquisitely wrought, and the designs were modest and aesthetically pleasing.

There were, however, inevitable forces that changed many facets of the trade. An expanding and more affluent population created a demand for more products of all kinds. Improved means of transportation and technological advances provided facilities for increasing production, but in the eyes of most connoisseurs the quality of the product was not improved. This diminishing quality can be attributed to a number of circumstances, but the fact that the product more rarely became the work of one man, laboring at his bench from sunrise to sunset, seems to have been responsible for some of the deterioration.

Although the pounding of a tankard or a teapot from one piece of metal was a procedure demanding skill and patience, the demand for these products seems to have been met and a reasonably adequate supply of objects was available for those who could afford to buy them in earlier times. It might be pointed out that the rewards for competent craftsmanship were rather high, and many craftsmen became fairly wealthy, holding positions of importance in their respective communities, as well as in the nation.

The most significant factor that brought basic changes to the trade was the introduction of rolled sheet silver, and the developments which arose from this innovation. The silversmiths no longer had to cast and pound his coins into sheets of suitable shape and thickness for the object he proposed to make; he could buy his sheet metal from a merchant, or a fellow craftsman who had the facilities for rolling sheet. (The high cost and infrequent use of rolling equipment did not warrant such a purchase by every silversmith.)

The following advertisement from the *Pennsylvania* (Philadelphia) *Packet*, October 23, 1789, focuses attention on the movement of events mentioned above. The contents of the advertisement indicate that, although some of the older tools continued to be in demand, a new era had arrived.

> The American Bullion and Refining Office, No. 1, Carter's alley, Second street,
>
> Is just opened for the purchase of old gold, silver, copper, brass, pewter and lead: the utmost value will be given for each of these articles; and as soon as a sufficient quantity can be collected, the refining will commence; also, the button, buckle, and plate manufactory when artists bred to any of these branches will receive liberal encouragement, and may be supplied with fine gold, silver, and flat-

ted metals. Wanted, the following tools and utensils; forging and raising hammers, triblets and beck irons; polishing wheels, collars and mandrels; ingots and skillets; a piercing press, a small anvil and spoon taste; moulds and screws; large and small weights, scales and vises; draw bench and plates; a large iron mortar and pestle. Persons having such articles, new or old, will receive a fair price, by applying as above.

Philadelphia, October 12.

To an observer of current and past events, it must be evident that the problems created by the easy availability of sheet silver were numerous and difficult to resolve. Silversmiths who were trained in the traditional way of making a silver vessel by raising it from a disk must have been very loathe to accept a procedure which looked like a "short cut," namely, the creation of a form with a joint from top to bottom. It is probable that the change was very welcome to those with more liberal views and a keener eye for favorable bank balances. One certainty of the situation is that on October 23, 1789, a refining office in Philadelphia advertised that craftsmen could "be supplied with fine gold, silver and flatted metals."

It is difficult for a person inexperienced in the making of metal objects to appreciate the catastrophic change this new method of fabricating brought to the trade. The workman no longer hammered and annealed for endless hours to obtain a flaring cylinder, for now by a method of drafting he could draw the shape, cut out the pattern, form the metal, and solder the joint in a small fraction of the time consumed to obtain the same result by the raising method.

A paragraph from *American Silver of the XVII & XVIII Centuries* by C. Louise Avery accurately describes the course of events and styles at that time. She tells that:

> The teapots by Revere and Schanck illustrate a style popular in England in the last quarter of the eighteenth century and much copied by contemporary American silversmiths. Sheet silver was rolled thin and shaped into oval, octagonal, or waved outline. The sides, of course, were vertical and the base flat. In the eighteenth century examples the spout is usually straight, the lid low and slightly domed. The contemporary scheme of decoration by bright-cut engraving was eminently suited to these formal but dainty shapes. The teapot was often accompanied by a stand on four feet.

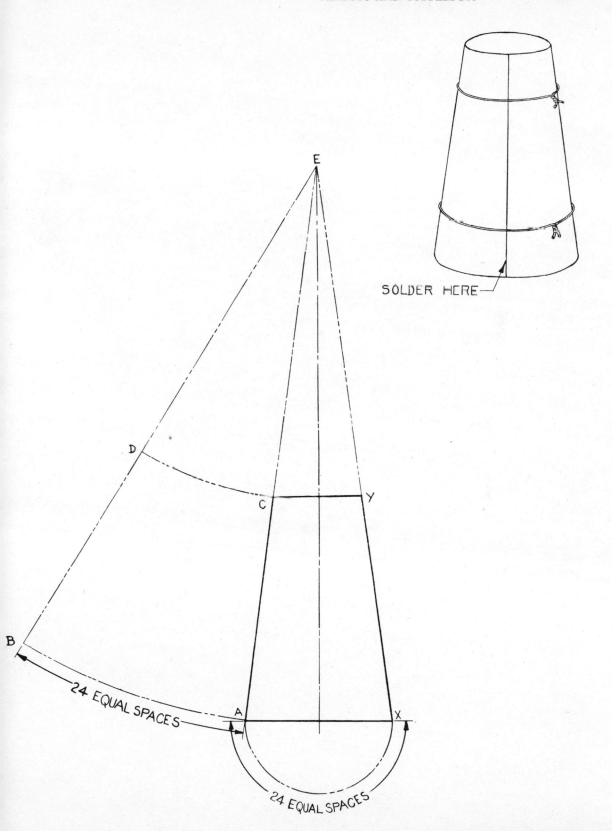

SOLDER HERE

24 EQUAL SPACES

24 EQUAL SPACES

A very elegant coffeepot made by Jacob Hurd, Boston, in the second half of the eighteenth century. This form could have been raised from a disk or made from a sheet with a joint under the spout or the handle. The latter method was used over a long span of time, but was most widely followed after rolled sheet became available. The lid was probably shaped in a swage. Height, 10¼ in. *Courtesy Henry Francis du Pont Winterthur Museum*

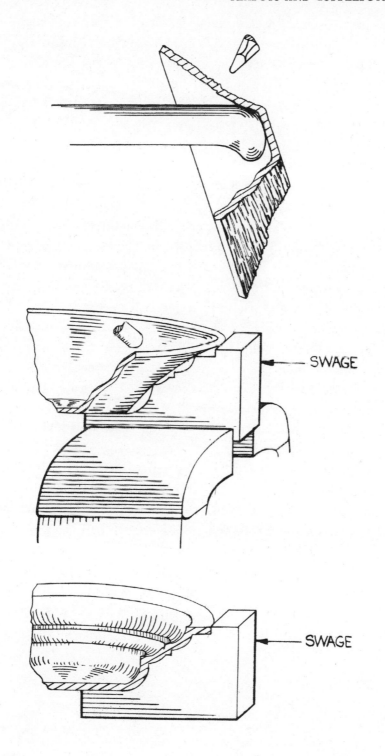

SWAGE

SWAGE

This description of a new style and its accompanying techniques must not lead the reader to think that all silversmiths immediately discarded the method of making hollow ware by raising, for some, particularly if they worked in areas less sensitive to change than the big cities on the seacoast, continued to remain competitive in the business and made attractive pieces. As a matter of fact, it is very evident that there was some hybridization in the trade, for the stretching and contracting techniques used for centuries on disks of silver were now used on some of the cylinders of metal created from thinner sheets of silver. It might also be noted that at least one form used a century earlier was revived and adapted to the classical pattern. The handles of wood used on such teapots and coffeepots closely resemble the one used by Coney on his pear-shaped teapot. Thus, it is very evident that silversmiths retained the practices which seemed best for hand methods of production, and discarded others when better ones came into general use.

It has been stated that at the beginning of the century silver was an expensive commodity; this situation caused objects made from it to be expensive and production was on a "piece-by-piece" basis for very evident reasons. Conditions changed slowly; in 1762 Mary Bartlett left two thirds of her estate to the third precinct of the Brookfield Church to be spent for silver vessels for the communion table on which both her name and that of her husband were to be engraved. This bequest resulted in the making of six silver tankards by Paul Revere, engraved as directed, and dated 1768.

Although the act of Mary Bartlett was evidence of some affluence, it hardly matches the elegance and grandeur seen in a tea and coffee service made by Joseph Richardson, Jr., in Philadelphia about 1790. Totaling nineteen pieces, the set includes a coffeepot (now distinctly differing from the teapots by its height and great over-all size), two teapots, a sugar urn, milk pot, waste bowl, tea tongs, and twelve spoons. With such evidence one can hardly dispute the fact that silversmithing and its prod-

Coffee and tea service made by Joseph Richardson, Jr., Philadelphia, about 1790. These objects are evidence of Philadelphia's rise to a position of leadership in the arts despite its late start in comparison with earlier settlements in New England and Virginia. Richardson obviously used both old and new techniques in making these vessels. *Courtesy Henry Francis du Pont Winterthur Museum*

1798
12th Mo 27

Samuel Richards . . . . is . . . . Cr
By Cash 66.19.5   75

Rachel Richards . . . . is . . Dr

To a fluted Silver Tea Pott wt 26.17
To a ditto . . Slop Bowl . 16.14
To a ditto . . Sugar Dish . 18.12
To 6 ditto 6 Table spoons 13.12   62.3 @ 18/ £55.18.7   carvd hands . 8..3..
To 12 ditto 12 Tea spoons . .6.14   ditto 4.16.2
To 2 ditto Sauce ladles . .3.12.12 ditto & fluted . . 2.15 —
To 1 Soup ladle . . . . .8.13.12 ditto . ditto . . 4.12.6
To 1 Silver Sugar tongs . . .1.6.12 . . . . . 1.11..
To 2 ditto Salt ladles . . . .11.12 . . . . . . .10.7
To 1 neat carvd Handle for Tea Pott 12.6
To 6 plain Tea Spoons . . .3.12.0 . . . . 2..2.6
To 1 ditto Table spoon . 1.13.12 . . . . 1..1.3

To engraving 3 Cyphers @ 7/6 . . £1..2.6
To ditto . . an 6 Table spoons 7.6
To ditto . . 18 Tea spoons 11.3
To ditto . . 1 Soup ladle . . . 2..
To ditto . . 2 Sauce ladles . . 2.6
To ditto . . Sugar tongs & Salts . 2.9
To ditto . . Cream Pott . . 5..
2..13.6   £84..9..7

Entries in the day book of Joseph Richardson, Jr., of Philadelphia in 1798 indicate that one order included most of the silver items for a dinner service. There are plenty of spoons and ladles, but no knives and forks. The cream pot (mentioned last) may have been intended as part of the tea service with a fluted pattern. *Courtesy Historical Society of Pennsylvania.*

ucts had reached its grandest era. Few products of the nineteenth century deserve the high commendation given to their predecessors.

Little need be said about the modes of fabrication in the "Classical Era." A logical variety was given to the shapes of vessels by making some with straight parallel sides, which were easy to form; while majestic coffeepots, along with holders for sugar and cream, were given vaselike forms, produced by the old method of raising a disk. A knowledge of coring might have permitted the smith to cast a spout for the coffeepot in one shell-like piece, the gallery was just another exercise in punching or drilling with subsequent filing, and the pineapple finials on the lids of the pots were cast and finished with files and gravers. The flaring base with its square bottom was fabricated from two pieces of metal and joined with solder and the entire base unit was attached to the body by the same method.

The tops and bottoms of the teapots with straight sides were cut out of a larger sheet with snips, the sides shaped over a round stake and fitted perfectly before the vertical joint was soldered. This joint was usually placed under the handle or the spout, as these were the most inconspicuous places to put it. The pattern for the spout was shaped by conical projection, and it also had a joint from end to end. The domed lid was shaped on the traditional tree trunk and made smooth with a planishing hammer on an appropriately shaped stake. After the object was assembled, it was polished and ready for the market place.

One facet of silversmithing in the Avery quotation, however, needs special attention, namely, the term "bright-cut." Authorities are usually vague in defining bright-cut, although the following description from *Three Centuries of English Domestic Silver,* seems to adequately describe how the glittering effect was achieved.

> Bright-cutting was at its most popular in the 1790's. It seldom appeared on spoons after 1800 but on tea services might be introduced as late as 1815, sometimes combined with other decoration. In this form of engraving the tool employed, in various sizes, was a gouge, sharpened chisel-wise, beveled from corner to adjacent corner and having two cutting points. Edge and point were used as required to produce what was really a kind of chip carving, outlining patterns of flowers, ribbons and so on by cutting narrow channels with variously slanting sides to produce the delicate faceted effect.

The final manner of creating hollow ware from rolled sheets of silver is succinctly described in *Old English Silver* by Judith Banister. She calls it "turning up from a cone."

> A less onerous method of making hollow-wares such as tankards and coffeepots, and one used at least since the seventeenth century, is to turn up the body from a cone of silver [sheet]. A suitably sized piece of silver is seamed to form a cylinder or cone, and then it is hammered to shape over a stake. The faint marks of the seam can often be detected inside the pot, usually along the line of the handle joints. In turning up from a cone, the process of corking [caulking] cannot be used, and a mouth wire and the base or foot must be soldered in.

It is unfortunate that the story about silversmiths of the eighteenth century does not end with a completely happy note; however, they were unquestionably the greatest artisans of America and their products attest to their achievements.

Other Objects

It was pointed out in the introduction that the major part of this survey would be devoted to the tools, techniques, materials, and products of the silversmith in America in the eighteenth century. As one proceeds with such an examination, the fact becomes evident that some objects of silver do not fit the matrix which has been planned, and that a larger scope must be created to give the reader as comprehensive an over-view of the subject as possible. Thus, the author is confronted with the problem of breaking down the subject matter into sections. Such a procedure is fraught with many pitfalls, for any division of the subject tends to make one section appear to be more important than another. In this case, the objects chosen for the previous sections were selected on the basis that they are important examples, and that their making involved many of the fundamental processes in the fabrication of objects of silver. There is no implication that they are the most important nor the most valuable.

Most of the objects included in this last section of the survey are found in well-known collections; however, no claim is made for this survey as being a complete coverage of the subject. Many unrecorded objects are located in small collections, and have received no public notice, but most of the well-known articles are described and often some comment is made about how they were fabricated, the latter facet being the major reason for this entire survey.

APPLE CORER

Only one example of this diminutive object has been found; it is in the Heritage Collection at Old Deerfield, Massachusetts. It consists of two principal parts, each of which are about the same length, the over-all

Apple corer of the early eighteenth century with the mark "T.H.," an unidentified maker. Some children were born with a silver spoon in their mouths, maybe some were born with a silver apple corer in their hands. *Courtesy The Heritage Collection, Old Deerfield, Massachusetts*

size being 5¾ inches. The handle appears to be turned from a solid piece of silver, to which is attached a number of knifelike blades to remove the core without the usual halving of the apple.

BASKETS

English baskets of the eighteenth century are usually round or elliptical, with or without a base, and have a semicircular handle attached by riveted joints which permit the handle to be raised or lowered. The bodies were created by the sinking and raising processes and usually are evidence of fine workmanship in shaping and piercing. The bodies have a lacelike quality due to the extensive piercings over most of the holding area.

At least two American baskets are known, both being in the Winterthur Collection. Both have rectangular shapes with rounded corners and no piercings. Both have applied bases made of strips of silver, one with

Basket by John McMullin, Philadelphia, about 1800. Insofar as many utensils for the table were made of silver, one would naturally think that such an object would have been very attractive for serving cake. Length, 12½ in.; width, 8⅜ in.; height, 3⅛ in. *Courtesy Henry Francis du Pont Winterthur Museum*

a three-ribbed molded edge at the bottom, while the other has a gadrooned border. Both are described as *cake baskets*.

BOXES

Boxes were usually small and used for carrying or storing such commodities as nutmeg, snuff, tobacco, sugar, and the like. They were made
in many shapes, the most common being square, round, rectangular, and
elliptical, with some being in the shape of a heart. Their small size suggests that they were designed to be carried in a pocket or a purse, and
their ownership was usually indicated by initials, which were beautifully
engraved on the lid.

The frugality of the silversmith in using small pieces of silver, left over from the
making of larger objects, created a perfect opportunity for him to make a small box.
This engraved snuffbox was made by Benjamin Brenton (1695-1749) in Newport,
Rhode Island, about 1725. The delicate motif engraved on the lid suggests that he was
a good engraver or had a good one do the work for him. Length, 2⅝ in.; width, 2 in.
Courtesy Henry Francis du Pont Winterthur Museum

There were, of course, exceptions to the usual sizes and shapes, one
of them being a sugar-box by John Coney. His product is elaborately
embossed and is mounted on a set of four legs with scrolled feet. The
lid is attached with a hinge, and a heavy ring of silver wire mounted on
the very top of the lid provides a satisfactory handle with which to
open the box.

Braziers are among the most decorative and useful objects made of silver for use on the table. Various ways have been devised to keep food warm while on the table and, obviously, a silver brazier was one of the most attractive means for this purpose. *Collection Philip Hammerslough*

BRAZIERS

The term "brazier" is interchangeably used with "chafing dish" when the object is made of silver for table use. It might be pointed out, however, that some large braziers made of brass are used in Spain and other countries in the Mediterranean area to provide a modicum of heat for an entire room.

The ones of concern here are made of silver, and resemble a bowl that is pierced to provide a draft for burning charcoal or a spirit lamp within, and are mounted on legs which also project beyond the top of the brazier. At the bottom the legs keep excessive heat from marring the top of the table. The extension above keeps the container in a horizontal position, and supports a vessel containing food. The earliest types were made completely of metal, but in the eighteenth century pads of wood were used on the bottoms of the legs to more fully protect the top of the table from the heat. Attractive handles of wood were also attached, so that they could be more easily managed at the table.

A piece with a similar function, called a dish ring, was made by Myer Myers, of New York, although his product lacked the spirit lamp, legs, and handle. The flaring circular band is pierced with interlacing cyma recta and cyma reversa curves, which provide a very interesting and rich decorative design and assist in dispersing the heat of the dish placed upon it, before much of it is conducted to the top of the table. In the middle of the delicate design motifs, a cartouche in the shape of a heart provides an attractive area for the engraving of three initials, possibly those of the owner.

BUCKLES

Knee-breeches buckles (at the knee) and shoe buckles were common products of the silversmiths. Often they were not made completely of silver, but were backed by other metals such as brass or bronze. The front surface of some were decorated with medallions of Washington.

BUTTONS

One would hardly look for such prosaic objects as buttons to be made of silver, but the elegant dress of the period doubtless warranted their use. Because of indifference, or their small size, few have survived.

Social customs always seem to have been subject to whims and fancies beyond the "call of duty." A silver buckle with medallions of Washington seem to fit such a category. *Courtesy Henry Francis du Pont Winterthur Museum*

Buttons by Peter Getz, who worked in Lancaster, Pennsylvania, toward the end of the eighteenth century. Although these objects seem very humble products for a silversmith, it should also be noted that Getz made some very elegant pieces also. *Courtesy Philip Hammerslough*

CANDLESTICKS

It is very evident from the scarcity of candlesticks in exhibitions and collections, that either very few of them were made, or very few have survived. This observation is confirmed in *American Silver of the XVII & XVIII Centuries* by C. Louise Avery, who says that:

> Candlesticks are comparatively rare in the Colonies, one of the very few examples of the earliest type being made by Dummer, now in a private collection. It follows the contemporary English style and has a square shaft representing clustered columns, square nozzle, and similar flange at the base of the shaft, and square moulded base.

This medieval style was used by other American silversmiths, one pair by Cornelius Kierstede being in the collection of the Metropolitan Museum, New York. The columns were formed by hammering sheets of silver into parts of a column and then soldering them together. They

Pair of candlesticks made by Samual Williamson, working in Philadelphia in 1794. The shaped baluster stems have reeding reminiscent of a similar procedure used on pewter objects made in Philadelphia at the same time. Height, 5¼ in. *Collection Philip Hammerslough*

were simply decorated by arranging the parts in an interesting manner, or by fluting and reeding. The bases are square or octagonal, and slightly raised to give a minimal decorative quality. Their molded edge was simply executed, however; an example made by Coney had its base ornamented by the gadrooning technique.

By the middle of the seventeenth century a baluster type stick, cast of silver, became popular in England. About a half century later this

Candlesticks were a very necessary household item in the nineteenth century, and are probably more prized now than they were then. They could be used on tables, stands, mantels, and window sills, for example, and all households had some, of one material or another. The faceted candlesticks by John Coney were presented to Tutor Henry Flynt by his students at Harvard University. They are very attractive, but not unique, for an English example is made in the same style. *Courtesy The Heritage Collection, Old Deerfield, Massachusetts*

style became popular in America, because it could be quickly cast of silver and, of course, they were fashionably compatible with other fittings of the household. Most of the baluster type are round; however, John Burt made an octagonal pair.

One of the most exciting pairs of baluster sticks is the pair made by John Coney, now in the Heritage Collection at Old Deerfield, Massachusetts. These are cast in a faceted design, which was much more difficult to execute than a round or octagonal one; however, the work seems warranted for the refracted light from its facets suggests a similar action from precious stones cut in this manner. The status of these candlesticks in the eyes of the owner is evident, for a photograph of them serves as a frontispiece in *The Heritage Collection of Silver* by Martha Gandy Fales and Henry Flynt.

Snuffers and trays of silver were also made by the craftsmen to serve with the sticks which they seem to have infrequently made.

CASTERS

The term "caster" seems to have been derived from the function of an object used to cast various substances through holes onto food. Despite the fact that salt was usually served from an open dish, it was also shaken

Casters were a pleasing adjunct to table accessories and a pair such as these were both attractive and useful. This pair was made by Benjamin Burt, Boston, about 1765. Height, 5⅛ in.; diameter of base, 1¼ in. *Courtesy Henry Francis du Pont Winterthur Museum*

Cruet stands, which contained casters among their assembly, are very elegant and doubtless were a scarce commodity in the eighteenth century. This stand was made by Daniel Christian Fueter, New York, about 1760. The casters bear the mark of a London silversmith for 1752. Height of stand, $9\frac{1}{16}$ in. *Courtesy The Heritage Collection, Old Deerfield, Massachusetts*

through a caster, as were other commodities such as pepper, sugar, and flour. Small casters were called "muffineers"; however, the word "muffineer" was often used to describe a dish for holding muffins.

Many of the early casters were straight-sided and round, although some were octagonal. They were usually fabricated from sheet silver

and have a vertical joint which is soldered with hard solder. More elaborate shapes appear in the eighteenth century in such shapes as vases, bal-
usters, and pears. The openings in the top were often highly ornamented,
and some have turned finials.

Some casters were integrated parts of cruet sets, which were very ornamental in table settings, not to mention their usefulness. Oil and vinegar
were usually added to the other condiments; however, the containers in
cruet sets were usually made of glass with silver tops and fitted into a
base made of silver. One cruet stand made by John David (1736-1798),
of Philadelphia, held glass containers with silver tops bearing the touch-
mark of a London silversmith.

CHALICES

Chalices are reported to have been the only ecclesiastical vessels of
silver never used for domestic purposes. Their function was to hold wine
in the communion service of the church. The chalice was passed to the
parishioners to take a sip as they sat in the pews or knelt at the altar.
This practice continues to be followed today, particularly by some of
the religious sects in Lancaster County, Pennsylvania, as well as many
others.

The top portion of most chalices was raised like a small bowl into
the shape of an inverted bell or vase and mounted on a thin stem with
a flaring base. An enlarged portion, called a knop, was often placed near
the center of the stem as a decorative device and to provide a firm grip
while using the object.

The narrow stem and base were fabricated from sheet silver, for it
would have been very difficult to raise such a slender form. The flaring
base was probably stretched from the metal used for the stem with a
cross-peen hammer over a stake. It was then planished and possibly a
small decorative edge was added by using a swage.

Some European examples have lids, which add to their decorative and
sanitary qualities.

CUPS (two-handled)

A number of two-handled cups have survived, but documented evidence about their use is rather confused and fragmentary. They were

an important object, however, for a photograph of one is used on the dust jacket of *An Introduction to Old English Silver* by Judith Banister, and one is prominently illustrated in *American Silver* by John Marshall Phillips with the following caption:

> The richness of the metal and beauty of form in the Queen style is enhanced by the finely cast handles and engraved ornamental inscription of this monumental two-handled cup by Jacob Hurd, a presentation piece of 1744, honoring an early naval victory in King George's War.

One in the Heritage Collection is low, resembling the traditional form of a caudle cup, with a molded base, two handles, and a lid with three projecting studs, which served as feet when the lid was inverted and used as a tray to hold the cup. It is highly ornamented with embossed designs around the lower portion reaching almost halfway up the side of the cup; the lid is ornamented in a similar manner. This one was a gift to Judith Bayard, when she was christened on December 13, 1698.

The term "grace cups" is used by Kathryn C. Buhler in her book entitled *American Silver,* although the implication of her terminology is not explained. It seems that their major purpose, and one which has survived until today, seems to have been to reward a person or organization for an outstanding act or achievement. In his book *Old Silver of Europe and America,* E. Alfred Jones supports the idea that the cup was used as a reward for an act of merit. He tells that:

> The two-handled cup and cover, 12⅜ in. high, now in the Essex Institute at Salem, was presented by the province of Massachusetts to Colonel Benjamin Pickman, a man of consequence in that old Massachusetts town, for his great services in promoting the famous expedition to Louisburg, also commemorated by some English caddies given to William Peperell, illustrated later. It was made by William Swan (1715-1754) of Worcester, Massachusetts, after some English cup as that by George Wickes of London, about 1730, once the property of the celebrated John Hancock and Illustrated in Mr. Bigelow's book (No. 117).

It seems to be abundantly obvious that these objects were of great importance, and, therefore, the quality of workmanship found in their construction indicates that they were skillfully produced. There was cer-

This handsome two-handled cup with cover is an extravagant display of the technique of the silversmith. Made by John Coney, it was presented to Harvard University by Governor William Stoughton, who died in 1701. The Stoughton arms are engraved on it. *Courtesy Fogg Art Museum, Harvard University.*

tainly some variation in the procedures used to make them, but the large upper portion was "raised" in the traditional manner of making hollow ware, as were the handles and bases. The example by Jacob Hurd is sparcely ornamented, the craftsman using the traditional combinations of curves and flat areas to produce the molded parts of the lid and the base. The natural S curve of the handles complements the simple charm of the body, and over-all it is one of the most charming pieces of American silver extant.

FISH SERVERS

Fish servers are in a different category from cutlery because they do not have a cutting edge. Many are in the shape of a fish (a very logical design), and most of them were ornamented by piercing and/or engraving. The handle is offset above the level of the table so that it could be easily grasped for use.

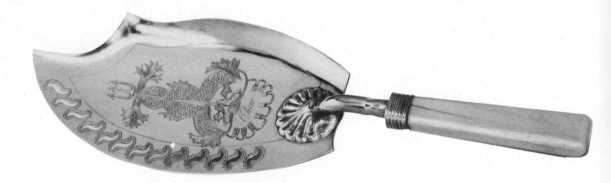

Fish servers frequently have the shape of a fish, but the silversmith who made this one seems to have been imaginative and created a different form. This one shows a number of the techniques of the silversmith such as piercing, engraving, and embossing. The handle of ivory is also a very attractive feature. *Collection Phillip Hammerslough*

GUNS

One of the most interesting and elusive areas of craftsmanship in silver is the work done on guns. The conclusions are different than with the workmanship on swords, for many of the men who did the silverwork on swords signed their products. The frustration in not being able to identify the craftsman who executed work in silver on guns is particu-

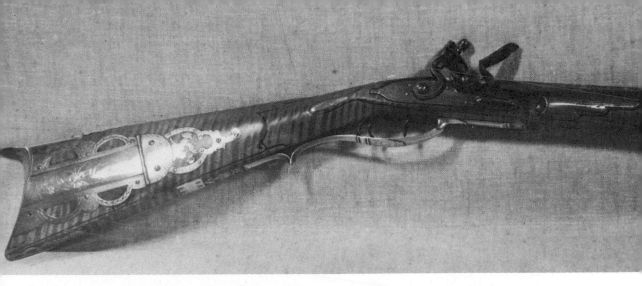

The reverse side (cheek side) of the Kentucky rifle with a patch box made of silver. The high quality of workmanship is not only evident in the inlaying of silver, but also in the carved designs in bas-relief and the design engraved on the large piece of silver in the center of the butt-end of the gun. *Alfred Clegg Collection.*

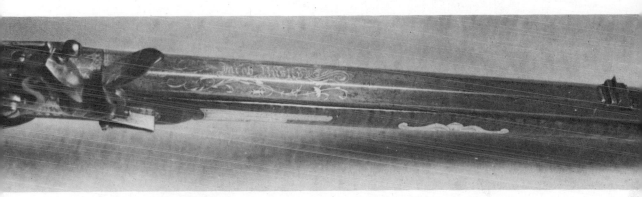

A Kentucky rifle with stock of curly maple and mounts of silver. The style of the various parts, such as the patch box and the trigger guard, suggests that the gun was made in the early years of the nineteenth century. The maker's name, Jacob Ruhlig, is inlaid with strips of gold in the top facet of the barrel. *Alfred Clegg Collection.*

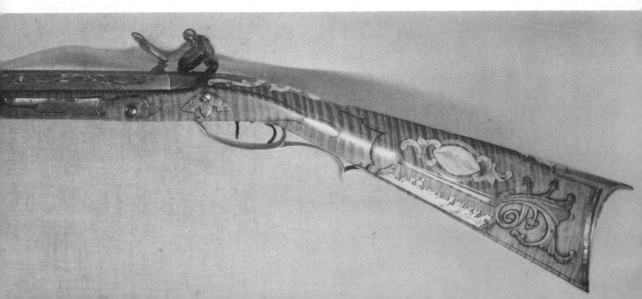

larly vexing because relatively few such guns exist, and their most attractive feature remains a matter of mystery.

There are a number of reasons for the uncertainty about the identity of the worker who produced the mountings of silver. It is generally agreed that in the early portion of the eighteenth century most of the work done on a gun was by one man, the gunsmith. He welded the barrel,

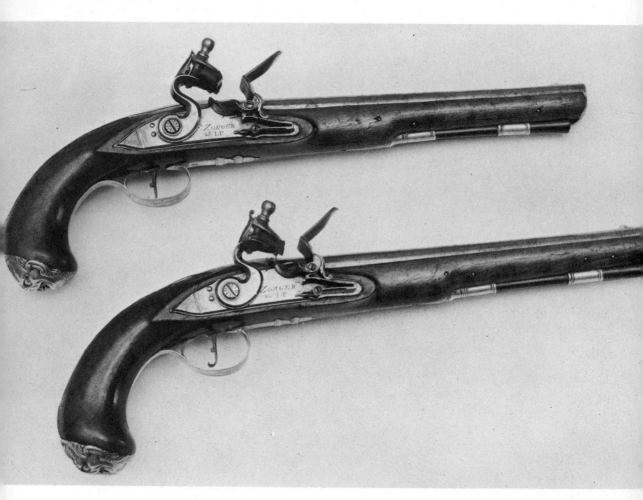

Pair of pistols made by Frederick Zorger (1734-1815), York County, Pennsylvania. It is thought that these pistols were made between 1765 and 1780, possibly for a member of the Continental Congress when it met in York. The stocks are of curly maple with silver mounts; i.e., stock butt plate with mask, trigger guard, and ramrod pipes. On the lock is inscribed "F. Zorger/& I.F.," and on the top of the barrel near the breech, "York Town," *Courtesy Henry Francis du Pont Winterthur Museum.*

cast the brass, carved the wood, and fitted the barrel. They were bleak days, however, and little, if any, silver is found on guns of this era, with perhaps the exception of a few silver inlays.

During the greater part of the eighteenth century the gun is thought to have been principally the product of the gunsmith, so if any silver-work is found on the gun, it is highly likely that he did it. There were, however, two alternatives to such an hypothesis. The gunsmith could have salvaged silver parts from a gun made in Europe and used them on one of his products without any commitment concerning the maker of the silver parts. He also could have "sub-contracted" the work in silver to an American silversmith who did not identify his product with his usual mark. Such a procedure could have been followed because the gun-smith did not wish to disclose the maker of the silver parts of the gun.

Near the end of the eighteenth century the situation regarding the making of metal parts for a gun changed, particularly in urban centers where large hardware stores were located. Advertisements appear in news-papers indicating that such stores sold gun mountings, and brass founders are known to have followed the same procedure. Specialization was also occurring among gunsmiths and some are known to have particular in-terest in making barrels, locks, and other parts.

This situation, combined with the rising affluence of the populace, created a demand for guns with silver mountings and many more inlays. The Winterthur Collection includes a pair of pistols with silver mount-ings made by Zorger, a gunsmith working in York, Pennsylvania, in the late eighteenth century. There are other examples of similar work; how-ever, the identities of the silver craftsmen remain anonymous.

One Kentucky rifle with a flintlock (of the nineteenth century) in the Clegg Collection in Birchrunville, Pennsylvania, is completely mounted with silver parts. This is probably one of the earliest and fin-est examples of such work in America, and the craftsman added the final flourish of using gold to inlay his name in the top facet of the octagonal barrel. Unfortunately, the identity of the silversmith is un-known; however, it is the writer's guess that the parts were made by the gunsmith.

In the percussion era of gunmaking the use of silver mountings be-came more common, particularly, when "presentation" pieces were made.

INDIAN MEDALS

It is a well-established fact in the history of United States that some questionable business transactions were conducted with the Indians when land was bought from them. There is also a suspicion that some transactions with the red men were influenced by the presentation of such gifts to them as guns and silver medals. The guns had an obvious function in the survival of the Indian, but the silver medals which were suspended around their necks by a chain had only a decorative value. These highly polished objects must have had a great appeal to the Indians and they were made over a long period of time. Although they did not constitute "hard money" in business transactions, it can readily be recognized that a few such medals judiciously distributed could create a favorable relationship between the two parties involved. They were usually the gift of a Governor or a President to persons who held prestigious positions among the Indian tribes.

The relationship between the white man and the Indian was a capricious one. The few surviving medals are evidence of one means the white man used to influence his neighbor. *Courtesy Henry Francis du Pont Winterthur Museum*

One is known showing an Indian dropping his tomahawk, and accepting a peace pipe from a white man. It cannot be said that the implied contract of peace was always binding on both parties; however, the medals are very romantic survival of colonial affairs in America.

Many of the earliest types were a simple form of sheet silver with appropriate subjects engraved on the surfaces of the silver. Some were made by Joseph Richardson, Jr., of Philadelphia, and Dan Carrel of Charleston, South Carolina, inserted the following advertisement in the *Charleston Gazette*, on July 25, 1791.

DAN CARREL
No. 129 Broad-street
Manufactures all kinds of silver, gold, and jewelry work. viz: silver Indian work, plate work, all kinds of spoons, buckles, small work, gold lockets, buttons, rings, etc. paintings, hair work, engraving, gilding, etc. The workmen he employs and his experience in the business, enables him to do most of the above work equal in every respect and cheaper than those imported. Cash or goods for old gold and silver.

The simplicity of these objects combined with the great demand for them has caused some unscrupulous craftsmen to make modern reproductions of them which have drifted into the market place and have been sold as genuine originals.

INKSTANDS

An early inkstand was called a "standish," the latter term being used until the middle of the nineteenth century. Only a few made by American silversmiths have survived, the most famous one, previously mentioned, being in Independence Hall, Philadelphia. It was made in 1752, by Philip Syng, Jr., in Philadelphia, and was used by the signers of the Declaration of Independence and of the Constitution. In recent years it has been on display where it was originally used.

The flat traylike portion of the object was probably made like a salver, although the flat surface in this case has been indented to hold the three containers on its top. The fit of these containers is so precise that even today considerable pressure is required to remove them from their shallow indentation. The three containers consist of one for ink, one for sand used to "dry" the ink, and one for the quills. There are holes in the

Inkstand made in 1752 by Philip Syng, Jr., of Philadelphia. Its importance was recognized early in the twentieth century for it was illustrated on a postcard, probably sold as a souvenir at Independence Hall. *Independence Hall Park Collection*

top of the quill holder into which quills were inserted when not in use, and its handle supported the holder when the quills were distributed to the signers.

Another example was made by John Coney (1655-1722), Boston, Massachusetts. This one has a triangular shape and the handle is attached to the tray instead of to the quill holder. The tray is mounted on three animals lying in a prone position, their raised heads seemingly holding the tray in its proper place.

LADLES

Ladles obviously have a close kinship with spoons. They were made in a similar manner, but in a variety of shapes and sizes. The bowls ranged from round to elliptical, and some were fluted like the one made by Samuel Edwards, now in the Winterthur Collection. Many of the fine examples have ferruled handles into which wood or ivory is attractively fitted.

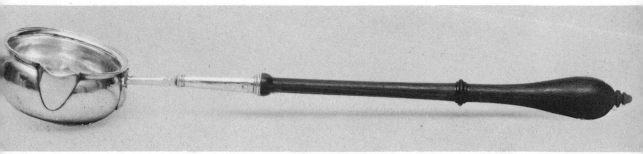

Ladles are among the most charming products of the American silversmith in the eighteenth century. Many are made entirely of silver. The handle of this one is particularly attractive because part of it is made of wood. It was made by Simeon Soumain (1685-1750) of New York, about 1725. *Courtesy Henry Francis du Pont Winterthur Museum*

NAILS

The role of a nail has been a very humble one in all civilizations which used them, and they are of more ancient origin than most men would suspect. There was a great variety in size and function of nails in the eighteenth century; however, little attention has been focused on those made of silver. There was probably a reasonably good demand for nails made of silver for they were not only functional, but highly decorative as well. Peter Getz, a silversmith working in Lancaster, Pennsylvania, obviously made some of silver for F. Stineman who was a local hardware merchant. The invoice includes a number of other items which were common commodities and procedures for a silversmith.

In the nineteenth century a Lancaster gunsmith named Melchior Fordney used silver tacks to ornament his rifles of the highest quality. Few men used silver tacks as imaginatively as Fordney, and the result was a very fortunate one. It should be noted that he used them entirely for decorative purposes.

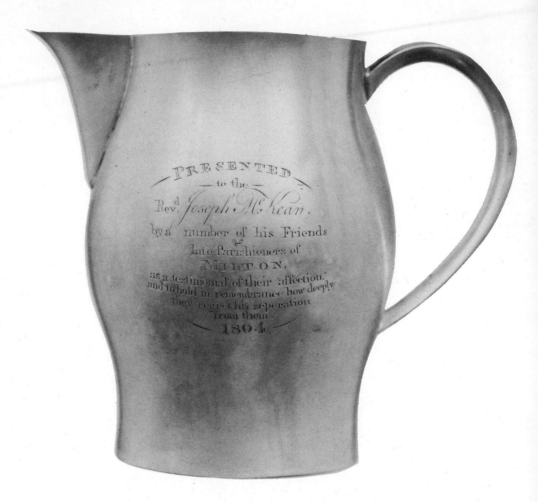

Pitchers were made in many shapes and sizes for a variety of purposes. There were small, pear-shaped ones for cream; late in the eighteenth century some larger examples simulated the shape of ceramic style commonly known as "Liverpool." This one was made by Paul Revere; the inscription indicates for whom made. *Courtesy Henry Francis du Pont Winterthur Museum*

PITCHERS

There was considerable variety in the size and shape of pitchers made of silver. Possibly the most attractive small form was made about the middle of the century in the inverted-pear shape, mounted on three legs, with a strap handle of silver. These were used principally for cream and, although none seems to match the design of contemporary teapots of the period, they are compatible and are often exhibited together.

The bodies were raised from a disk of silver, like most of the hollow ware of the period, and are usually fine examples of craftsmanship. Their small size confronted the silversmith with a challenge in the raising procedure, much more than a larger teapot or bowl. The cabriole legs were cast and attached by soldering them to the body. The handle was attached by a similar method.

Larger pitchers made in the late eighteenth century sometimes had covers and were possibly used for cider or other drinks. A form very much copied in silver and pewter was made by Paul Revere in 1804 and was inspired by the ceramic pitchers made in Liverpool. The bulbous center recedes in diameter almost equally toward the top and the bottom. The lip is attached and the handle appears to be made of a piece of tubing not very attractively shaped, but quite functional in its relationship to the vessel.

SALTS

Containers for salt fall principally into two categories. One is a closed caster as has been previously described, the other being a circular open dish from which salt was removed with a small spoon. The common salt dish was really a small bowl mounted on three legs, somewhat in a cabriole form with a hoof pattern at the base.

Another dish type was mounted in a circular shell which has a noticeable flare outward toward the base. This type is regarded as the earliest and usually is very modestly decorated.

Open salt made by A. Carman, working at Kingston, New York, in 1770. *Courtesy Henry Francis du Pont Winterthur Museum*

SALVERS

The terms "salver" and "tray" are interchangeably used today to describe the same object, and in reality they serve the same function, namely, the serving of food or drinks. In style they range from a circle with a simply molded edge to a slightly more elaborate form with a cast edge soldered to a flat sheet of silver, and finally, to trays with very elaborately scalloped edges resembling the form of the piecrust edge of a tilt-top table. One of the latter type was made by Paul Revere and would be regarded as an extravagant design by any standards. Revere also made an oval example with a molded edge which included two handles. Such appendages are rarely found on salvers made of silver.

There were many designs of salvers by many makers. This one was made by Jeremiah Elfreth, Jr. (1723-1765), about the middle of the eighteenth century. *Courtesy Philadelphia Museum of Art*

One of the most attractive examples, made by Thomas Edwards of Boston (1701-1755), is virtually a square form with a concave cutout in each corner. The simply molded edge is enhanced by a design engraved next to it on the bottom surface of the tray.

SAUCEBOATS

Although sauceboats were used in Europe long before they became fashionable in America, it is interesting to note that the American examples are regarded as the most attractive by some connoisseurs. They usually have oval bodies with a shaped edge and a long lip or spout. The open, double-scrolled handles resemble similar handles on other objects, but on sauceboats they are fastened only at the bottom, instead of at

One of a pair of sauceboats by Christopher Hughes, working in Baltimore 1771-1790. The initials "D E G" stand for their owner, Daniel E. Grant, who owned the Indian Queen Tavern and later the Mountain Inn of that city. The lack of silver articles in the Federal style suggests that Hughes was not very productive in his later life. He died in 1824. *Courtesy Old Salem, Inc., Winston-Salem, North Carolina*

Sauce pan with lip, cover, and turned handle of wood, made by J. Richardson, Jr., Philadelphia (1793-1815). This style shows a new trend from the earlier raised bulbous pattern. The cover is an attractive feature not usually found in earlier examples. *Courtesy Philadelphia Museum of Art.*

the top and the bottom, as they usually are. The sauceboats are mounted on four legs with designs peculiar to the craftsman who made them. One by John David has a shell motif on the foot as well as at the top of the leg where it is attached to the body of the sauceboat.

The bodies were probably started by the tensional stretching technique because it is easily used on objects that are not circular. After some depth was obtained by this method, additional depth could be obtained by inverting the form and placing it over a stake and striking the outside with a cross-peen hammer. The entire piece had to be planished to regain a smooth, slightly faceted surface. The legs were cast and attached with hard solder, as was the handle.

They were made widely in America by silversmiths working along the seaboard from Boston to New York, Philadelphia, and Baltimore.

SAUCEPANS

Saucepans were relatively small, in comparison with sauceboats, and served a different function. They are usually round with a bellied form reaching its greatest diameter near the bottom. They have short lips or spouts, and long handles mounted at a right angle to the spout. The handle consists of a metal ferrule attached to the body of the pan, into which a turned piece of wood is fitted. It is thought they were used to heat and serve a brandied sauce.

SKEWERS

Old skewers of any metal are scarce items today and, because relatively few were made, those of silver are among the scarcest. They look like long, flat nails with an opening in the larger end to assist in inserting and removing them from the meat. Their function was to attach the meat to a spit, as the spit rotated before the open fire on the hearth.

SPOUT CUPS

Spout cups are usually small, bulbous-bodied objects with slender handles and a small, curved spout, seemingly pressed tightly against the body of the vessel. Their principal use is thought to have been for feeding children, but they might also have been used for serving such drinks as tea or coffee.

Spout cups are possibly one of the less attractive products of the silversmith; however, their number indicates they had a very useful function. This one was made by John Dixwell of Boston late in the seventeenth or early in the eighteenth century. *Courtesy Henry Francis du Pont Winterthur Museum*

STRAINERS

Strainers are charming small objects designed to be placed over the top of vessels to remove any unwanted substance from liquids poured through them. They were usually circular and simply shaped small bowls with many holes providing the straining function. They were kept in position by two handles, mounted near the top on opposite sides of the bowl.

SWORDS

Although other objects of silver, or partially of silver, were produced through the combined efforts of a silversmith and a craftsman in another media, the division of work between them was in no case more precise than in the making of silver hilts (handles) for swords. The rea-

A silver-hilted sword was obviously evidence of luxury and stature in the eighteenth century. Few complete scabbards have survived. This one is stamped " J. Bailey, Fecit." *Courtesy Philadelphia Museum of Art; photograph by A. J. Wyatt staff photographer*

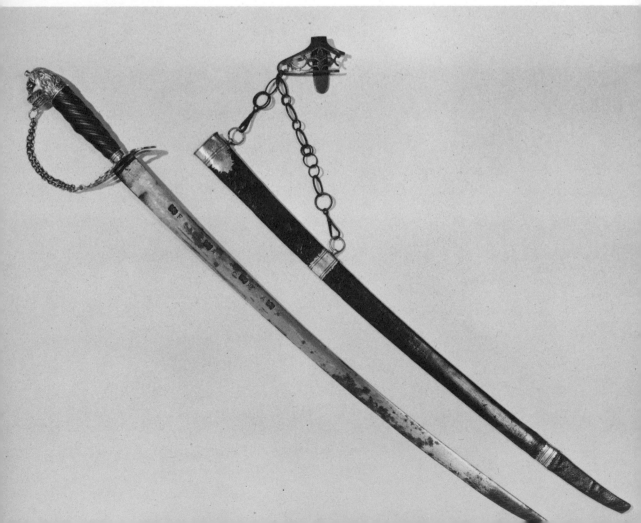

son for the division is easily evident. The making of the hilt involved the casting of silver from a pattern of the appropriate design and for ease in handling. The making of the blade required the skill of a cutler, or blademaker, for it was forged of steel. Forging iron was an everyday experience for a blacksmith, but the forging of steel required a keen sensitivity to the problems involved lest all the carbon be burned out of the steel and the blade lose its elasticity.

Tea caddy made by Joseph and Nathaniel Richardson, working in Philadelphia, 1771-1791. This caddy is of great interest to the technologist because the metal used to make the body was salvaged from an earlier object made of silver. An old and muchworn monograph remains on the inside surface. *Courtesy Philadelphia Museum of Art; photograph by A. J. Wyatt, staff photographer*

TEA CADDIES

A tea caddy of this period might logically be expected to be a part of a complete tea service, and this one could have been. However, it is also possible that a family could afford only a caddy and thus used it with objects of china, or regarded it most highly for its ornamental quality. It is interesting to note that this precious commodity of tea was secured by a lock. It should also be noted that the lock was fastened with rivets rather than soldered to the inside surface of the body of the caddy.

TEAKETTLES

The design of teakettles usually followed that of the contemporary teapot, or vice versa; however, there were some differences in the location of the spout and the handle. In the eighteenth century they were globular, pear-shaped, or in the shape of an inverted pear. The lids were attached by a hinge and one made by Jacob Hurd has a knob made of ivory, which is both attractive and very functional because of its non-conduction of heat.

They were supported on a band of silver which was raised from the level of the table by three or four legs, providing space for a spirit lamp to boil the water in the kettle. Tea was not brewed in the kettle (quite a misnomer) but water was heated and poured into the teapot.

Teakettles are rare items, possibly because they were very difficult to make, and the resulting cost so high that only a few affluent families could afford one.

TEA URNS

Late in the eighteenth century when the classical urn shape became very popular, tea urns replaced teakettles. The urn was mounted on a flaring round base, which in turn was soldered to a square form with feet at each corner. A small faucet was attached at the bottom of the urn for dispensing hot water. It it thought that at times tea instead of hot water was placed in the urn.

THIMBLES

A thimble is defined in *A Dictionary of Arts, Manufactures, and Mines* by Andrew Ure, New York, 1865, as:

A small truncated metallic cone, deviating a little from a cylinder, smooth within, and symetrically pitted on the outside with numerous rows of indentations, which is put upon the tip of the middle finger of the right hand [how about left-handers?], to enable it to push the needle readily and safely through cloth or leather, in the act of sewing. This little instrument is fashioned in two ways; either with a pitted end, or without one; the latter, called the open thimble, being employed by tailors, upholsterers, and generally speaking, by *needle-men*.

Thimbles were made by cutting silver into strips the desired size of the flat portion and formed into a band; this was joined with hard solder. A dome was stamped by using a concave and convex tool, between which

Thimble, decorated with foliated borders and two cupids holding a cartouche for a monogram (which has worn off or was never engraved). The name "I. BVRT" is placed above the border of the thimble Height, ¾ in.; diameter, 1⅛ in. *Courtesy The Historical Society of York County (Pennsylvania)*

a small disk of metal was placed and the convex one struck with a hammer. The two parts were joined with silver solder. The pits were created with a tool bearing protrusions, the inside of the thimble being previously fitted tightly to a mandrel to prevent the indentations from creating uncomfortable projections there.

TONGS

Two types of tongs were used to handle lumps of sugar in the eighteenth century. One was a simple strip of metal bent into the shape of a U with shaped finials on each end to grasp the sugar. The form of the ends was often similar to a small teaspoon which was obviously very functional and added a decorative quality to the object. The spring-like quality of these tongs was created by hammering the silver on a steel stake.

Another type of tong had an action like that of blacksmith's tongs,

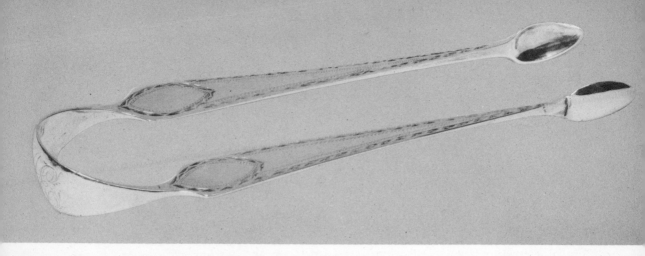

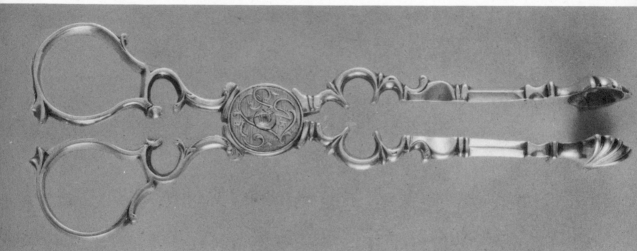

The tea tongs are part of the nineteen-piece tea and coffee service made by Joseph Richardson, Jr. They are an extremely clever example of craftsmanship in silver The scissors-like tongs are also beautifully executed but in an extremely different manner. They were made by Charles Oliver Bruff of New York. Length, 5 in. *Courtesy Henry Francis du Pont Winterthur Museum*

but more nearly resembled the shape of a small scissors. The two members were elaborately contoured from the handles to the ends of the tongs. A circular portion at the hinge was beautifully engraved on one example made by Charles Oliver Bruff (1735-1785), who worked in New York and advertised that he made "tea tongs" (sugar tongs).

TUREENS

A tureen is usually described as a large vessel used on the table for serving soup. They are, of course, very common in porcelain and pottery, but quite rare in silver. Some were made by raising a disk in a process similar to the making of a bowl (which they really are) and were provided with handles and a lid. Some were probably equipped with a tray and a ladle, appendages which were useful for the serving of soup.

One of the outstanding tureens is in the Hammerslough collection and was made by Peter Getz, of Lancaster, Pennsylvania. The lid is highly domed and richly ornamented, terminating in a finial which served as a knob for removing and replacing the lid.

This soup tureen was made by Peter Getz of Lancaster, Pennsylvania, about 1780 for Aaron Levy, of Philadelphia and Lancaster, whose ownership is indicated by the script capital L in the octagonal medallion underneath the engraved bowknot. It has a round convex body on a spreading molded foot. The loose, domed, overhanging cover has original repoussé work decoration. Poppy-bud handle surmounts poppy-leaf base; two ring handles have shell motif and are hinged on body below rim. Height, 8¾ in.; diameter, 7 in. *Courtesy Philip Hammerslough*

MISCELLANEOUS

The cross-section sampling which this survey has made of many collections in America focuses attention on the fact that none is really complete. This condition exists because no collector or museum could have access to all types of objects over the short span of years they have been collecting, and also because examples of all the work done by silversmiths have not survived. A scrutiny of the day books of Joseph Richardson, Jr., and Joseph Richardson, Sr., of Philadelphia shows that in addition to many of the enumerated objects in this survey they made the following items:

Baking dishes	Pap boats
Bells	Pap spoons
Bodkins	Pincushion loops
Breast pins	Scales
Chains	Sconces
Cloak hooks and eyes	Seals
Double-jointed tea tongs	Shoe clasps
Drinking tubes	Silver ferrols (ferrules)
Earrings	Spectacle frames
Girdle buckles	Spring boxes
Hairpins	Stock buckles
Hooks and eyes	Tweezers
Locket chains	Whip heads
Milk pots	Whistles
Pannikins	Wine cocks

They also repaired hundreds of objects. Many of them they doubtless made; however, one might suspect that many were imported and some were made by other craftsmen who no longer lived in the city of Philadelphia, or possibly had died; for, contrary to procedures today, the obsolescence of these objects was unlimited. They were designed to serve for generations, and obviously many of them did.

One can assume that silversmiths living in New York, Boston, Newport, or Charleston did a similar range of work, with some variations, and thus the total output of the American silversmith in the eighteenth century staggers the imagination of anyone who understands the tedious and slow processes involved in the daily work of this important artisan.

Summary

Many facets are involved in making a survey of a culture at any particular time. Such an observation is particularly true of this survey of techniques used by the eighteenth-century silversmith in America when objects were produced by hand methods. Such elements as time, style, economic conditions, and foreign influences are only a few of those which plague the author and complicate the hypotheses.

For example, no one knows when the first object was made, by whom it was made, or where. The culture of the seventeenth century was not blessed with initials such as I.B.M. and records are meager even for the most thickly populated areas such as Boston, New York, Philadelphia, and Charleston. Fortunately, some personal diaries, ledgers, and church and civil accounts survive from the eighteenth century which are very beneficial in some facets of the survey, but of little help in technology which is its major purpose. As a matter of fact, items such as style and place of origin were very vaguely regarded here until the twentieth century, and today uncertainty exists about when and where some objects of silver were made.

The normal procedure for the technologist is to look to European sources, which are very valid in evaluating American technology for all of the first craftsmen came from Europe. The system of apprenticeship perpetuated European practices for at least one generation in America and because they were so refined and highly developed they were not easily discarded. European influences are not only evident in silversmithing, but also in other trades such as gunsmithing, papermaking, and so on.

One of the most difficult problems to resolve in a technological survey is to determine when one practice was dropped and another substituted. As a matter of fact, one can virtually say that some were never discontinued for, at the moment, they seem to be beyond improvement. In one room of a big present-day manufacturer of silverware not one machine is to be found and, curiously, the work which was at one time done almost entirely by men is now done by women. Admittedly, the light for working is a little brighter than it was in the eighteenth century. In another room of the same manufacturer are tools once operated by hand power, but virtually identical tools are now motivated by tireless electric motors. The factory continues to produce unique objects and one can truthfully say that the virtues of production by hand methods are still very evident. Fortunately, or unfortunately, depending on the economy and the whims of the buyer, most objects of silver today are produced rapidly in identical patterns and it is for this reason that this effort has been made to preserve a knowledge of the techniques of the past.

Although no precision in dating can be made in such a survey, it has been the intent of the author to give some chronological sequence to the contents of the book. Comment has been made that the earliest pieces made in America were medieval in character and were compatible with the architecture and furnishings of the church and the house. Although some of these objects were ornamented, the forms were relatively simple, and could be made with a few tools. The sophisticated styles of mid-eighteenth-century England soon came to American shores, and American craftsmen were competing with "imports" in style and workmanship. In addition, they had a rapidly rising sense of national patriotism on their side, and eventually a craft of silversmithing was flourishing in America.

Many of their products are handsome, some are elegant, and few people know how they were made. The reader of this book will get some insight into this fascinating aspect of the craft, and thus become a more perceptive student of some of America's finest products of the eighteenth century.

Selected Readings

Avery, C. Louise, *American Silver of the XVII & XVIII Centuries*. New York, Metropolitan Museum, 1920.

Banister, Judith, *English Silver*. New York, Hawthorne Books, Inc., 1965.

——— *Old English Silver*. London, Evans Brothers, Ltd., 1965.

Bigelow, Francis Hull, *Historic Silver of the Colonies and its Makers*. New York, Macmillan, 1917.

Buhler, Kathryn, *American Silver in the Museum of Fine Arts, Boston*. Boston, Boston Arts Museum.

Clarke, Hermann Fredrick, *John Coney, Silversmith*. Boston, Houghton, Mifflin, 1932.

Colange, L., *Zell's Popular Encyclopedia*. Philadelphia, T. Ellwood Zell, 1871.

Diderot, Denis, et al., *Encyclopédie, Dictionaire des Sciences, Recueil des Planches, sur les Sciences, les Artes Liberaux, et les Artes Méchaniques*, 12 vols. Paris, Briasson et al., 1763.

Fabroni, Giovanna Valentine Mattia, *Diary of a Visit to England, with sketches of Machinery, Locks, Manufacturing Processes, etc.*, 1778-1779.

Fales, Martha Gandy, *American Silver in the Henry Francis du Pont Winterthur Museum*. Winterthur, Delaware, 1958.

——— and Flint, Henry N., *The Heritage Collection of Silver*. Old Deerfield, Mass., The Heritage Foundation, 1968.

Forbes, Esther, *Paul Revere and The World He Lived In*. Boston, Houghton Mifflin, 1942.

The Handy Book for Manufacturers. New York, Handy & Harman, 1955.

Hughes, Bernard and Therle, *Three Centuries of English Domestic Silver 1500-1820*. New York, Praeger, 1968.

Jones, E. Alfred, *Old Silver of Europe and America*. Philadelphia, J. B. Lippincott, 1928.

McLanathan, Richard B. K., ed., *Colonial Silversmiths, Masters and Apprentices*. Boston, Museum of Fine Arts, 1956.

Phillips, John Marsgall, *American Silver*. New York, Chanticleer Press, 1949.

Pleasants, J. Hall, and Sill, Howard, *Maryland Silversmiths*. Baltimore, Lord Baltimore Press, 1930.

Prime, Mrs. Alfred Coxe, *Three Centuries of Historic Silver*. Philadelphia, Pennsylvania Society of the Colonial Dames of America, 1938.

Schwahn, Christian, *Workshop Methods for Gold- and Silversmiths*. New York, Chemical Publishing Company, Inc., 1960.

Wenham, Edward, *The Practical Book of American Silver*. Philadelphia, J. B. Lippincott, 1949.

White, Benjamin, *Silver, Its History and Romance*. London, Hodder and Stoughton, 1917.

Index

(Italics refer to pages of illustrations)